Introduction

There is something positively epic – some might say, heroic – about moving huge loads on the public highway. And whilst it is incredible to think that more than 100 years ago Wynns achieved some amazing feats using little more than horse and muscle power, who can fail to be stirred by the sheer breathtaking, awe-inspiring sight of seeing maybe four powerful tractors moving a piece of electrical equipment or chemical plant the size of a block of flats?

It was as far back as 1890 that Robert Wynn had seen the need for a wagon that could move a 40-ton ships' boiler... a weight that was unheard of at the time. And it was almost certainly the lessons learned during those pioneering days that saw Wynns shifting larger and larger loads. But it was probably the ingenuity of Robert's son Percy – known generally as 'HP' – that led to the period that might be considered as Wynns' glory days in heavy haulage.

In the three decades following the end of World War 2 'HP' was responsible for Wynns staying ahead of the game by exploiting advances in technology to shift ever more impressive loads.

'HP' saw to it that Wynns acquired a fleet of war-surplus Diamond T tractors. The American Diamond T was designed for hauling 40-45-ton tank transporter trailers but, with its powerful Hercules diesel engine, this incredible truck could have been purpose-made for transporting the heavy electrical equipment that the Central Electricity Generating Board was installing in new power stations up and down the country. And if the exploits of Wynns' Diamond T fleet became the stuff of legend, they were certainly eclipsed by the second generation of war-surplus tractors – the mighty Pacifics which gave more than two decades of incredible service before these, too, were superseded, this time by Scammell's mighty 240/250-ton Contractor.

'HP' was also responsible for encouraging Cranes of Dereham to fit pneumatic tyres to a 150-ton trailer, that it was at Wynns' risk. It was also 'HP' who saw the benefits of trailers that were fitted with hydraulic steering and suspension, removing the need for a second tractor at the rear to assist with manoeuvring the load.

By the time Wynns celebrated its centenary in 1963, the company had acquired a 300-ton 48-wheeled trailer suitable for the largest loads of the period but loads continued to grow in size and weight and, by the middle of the next decade, Wynns had really shown what the technology of the day could do when a Scammell Contractor moved a 1,400-ton module 500 yards at Middlesborough Docks, before it was off-loaded using the trailer hydraulics.

Wynns' glory days may be behind them, but this does not diminish the incredible achievements of the past... Wynns truly were the pioneers of heavy haulage.   •

Pat Ware
October 2010

Although just two are visible, it required three Scammell Contractors to haul this 340-ton chemical vessel, the largest of 19 brought to the then new Texaco refinery at Pembroke in 1980. The lead tractor is brand new and has yet to be painted in the Wynns' livery.

Published by
KELSEY PUBLISHING LTD
Printed by William Gibbons on behalf of
Kelsey Publishing Ltd, Cudham Tithe Barn, Berry's Hill, Cudham, Kent TN16 3AG
Tel: 01959 541444 Fax: 01959 541400 Email: kelseybooks@kelsey.co.uk Website: www.kelsey.co.uk
©2010 **ISBN: 978-1-907426-13-1**

Contents

Pioneers of heavy haulage

John Wynn was born in October 1932, the son of George ('OG') Wynn, and great-grandson to Thomas Wynn who, in 1863, had founded a haulage company to distribute flour from the premises of the Star Flour Mills in Newport into the bakeries and shops in the South Wales valleys. Thomas Wynn died in 1878, but the business passed to his son Robert, the eldest of ten children, of which just two were boys.

Robert also had ten children, eight boys and two girls. Two of the boys died in infancy but, as soon as they were old enough, each of the surviving Wynn brothers joined their father to become involved in the family business. Each had his particular area of expertise... John's father, 'OG' was responsible for the administration of the business, which didn't interest John at all. John was far more interested in the heavy haulage and engineering side of the business, which was run by his Uncle Percy – 'HP' Wynn.

From an early age, John had spent much of his spare time at the company yard in Newport, South Wales and

It all comes down to horsepower... by the turn of the 20th Century there was stabling for 200 horses at Wynns' Shaftesbury Street premises and the use of horses continued until the end of World War 2.

Dreadnought was perhaps the most famous of Wynns' iconic Pacific tractors. It entered service in September 1950 and was later rebuilt with Scammell Contractor components and re-registered NDW 345G.

Thomas Wynn (1821-1878), the man who started it all.

had actually been driving – illegally – since the age of 12 or 13, much preferring this to school sports! He had already driven a six-wheel Scammell trunker down from London at night after the Commercial Motor Show and, without his father or his Uncle Percy's knowledge, every Saturday for a period of three or four months had been driving a Scammell articulated tanker loaded with sulphuric acid from the Wynns depot to Treforest, Pontypridd and back on a Saturday afternoon, a round trip of 40 miles. When this was discovered, he was 'grounded' by Percy and the official driver of the truck involved almost lost his job. As a

Robert Wynn (1863-1923). The son of Thomas, it was Robert Wynn who gave his name to the business.

In 1963, Wynns celebrated 100 years of business. This Fowler 30-ton road locomotive, dating from July 1920, formed part of a parade through the streets of Newport.

punishment, John was not allowed out in a Wynns' vehicle for the next 12 months unless Percy or Gordon Wynn were around to give the nod.

But, unbeknown to the young John, his father and uncle were aware that John had been driving vehicles around the yard and, without telling John, had asked a Zurich insurance inspector to quietly check up on his skills. Following this unofficial driving test, John was declared not to be an insurance risk and was allowed to continue with his under-age driving... but only whilst on private property. When he reached the legal driving age, he regularly took a hand at the wheel and was not averse to taking the driving seat of the Scammell Contractors... developing

skills that would never desert him.

It was obvious that John's first love was driving. It is fortunate that, from the age of 16, he was taken under the wing by his Uncle Percy because Percy's patronage saved John from what he believed would be a life of tedium in the office and allowed him to be part of the 'sharp end' of the business. Frequently acting as Percy's driver, he was presented with the perfect opportunity of picking the older man's brains during the long hours

they spent together in the car in those distant days before motorway travel reduced journey times.

There is little doubt that John was able to acquire unsurpassable knowledge and hands-on experience of moving abnormal loads during his long involvement with the company. Along with his cousin Noel, John was voted to the Board of Wynns in 1960. Both of them stayed with the business following the sale to United Transport in 1964.

Robert Wynn & Sons was formed in 1923 and was run by five Wynn brothers, generally known by their initials; from left to right, standing, HP, OG, RT, Alan, GP; seated, Hilda, Sam, and Emma. Alan, Hilda and Emma were not involved in the business.

Steam power diminished in importance during the 1930s as diesel- and petrol-engined trucks became ever more capable.

Wynns were responsible for hauling two 100-ton naval guns from Shoeburyness to London, and for placing them at the entrance to the Imperial War Museum.

A youthful John Wynn posing with a rare Austin A70 Hereford pick-up.

John Wynn with his two sons, Robert (left) and Peter (right).

United Transport was becoming a big player in the transport sector and, since 1956, some 20 per cent of the company had been owned by the large British industrial conglomerate known initially as the British Electric Traction Company, but subsequently renamed BET plc in 1985. BET increased their stake in United Transport to 100 per cent in 1971 which meant that they now effectively owned Wynns, Wrekin Roadways, and Sunters of Northallerton. Both Sunters and Wrekin Roadways had originally been competitors to Wynns, but the recession of the early '80s had seen both of them both merged with Wynns under the name United Heavy Transport.

At this point, although John remained with the business – at least for a while – Noel opted for early retirement. He subsequently was voted chairman of the Road Haulage Association (RHA), county chairman of the Confederation of British Industry (CBI), and a fellow of the Chartered Institute of Logistics and Transport (CILT), as well as being a member of the national and Wales councils of the CBI. Noel passed away, aged 87, on 12 May 2008.

John hated the big business ethos of BET and his increasing frustrations with the company's management style led to his resignation in June 1982, after 34 years with the company which his great-grandfather had founded. It is ironic perhaps that although the Wynns name soon disappeared from the trucks, BET retained the transport business of United Transport for the next decade, but the company was eventually acquired by Rentokil in a hostile take-over bid in 1996. Now trading as Rentokil Initial, aside from offering courier services, the company has no transport interests at all whilst, on the other hand, the Wynn family is back in heavy haulage through John's son Peter.

John Wynn was never to escape the reputation for moving heavy loads which he had helped Wynns to acquire and, through a lifetime's involvement with heavy haulage, which continues to this day, has become something of a legend among transport enthusiasts. •

Robert and Peter Wynn pose with John's mother Margery in front of one of the famous Pacific tractors.

Photographed in April 2009, Peter, John and Robert Wynn. Peter continues to run Robert Wynn & Sons, albeit now concentrating on moving outsized loads on water.

The early days

A 5-ton Garrett steam engine, new in 1915 and acquired by Wynns in 1921, double-heads a 5-ton Fowler dating from 1921. The load is a 26-ton boiler on a solid-tyred trailer.

It must have been extraordinary to live in Great Britain in the 19th Century. Was there ever a time that created such a roll-call of honour and achievement? Consider some of the names – Isambard Kingdom Brunel, Robert Stephenson, Joseph Bazalgette, and Joseph Locke (the latter not to be confused with the tenor Josef Locke).

Looking back at them now, they seem to be archetypal Victorians; men of enterprise, energy, talent and social responsibility. They understood what Great Britain lacked and, in a whirlwind of engineering brilliance and ability, created an infrastructure that we're still living with today – railways, tunnels, sewers, pumping stations, bridges, and viaducts. There must have been something in the Victorian air that made such men. And, in his own way, Thomas Wynn was another of these 19th Century heroes.

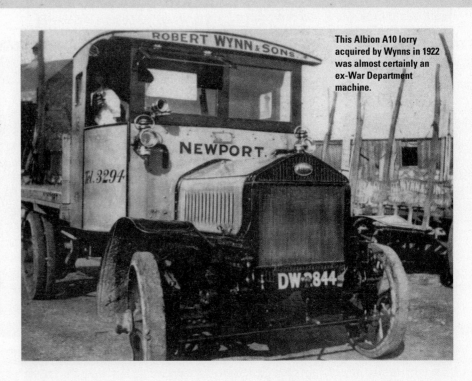

This Albion A10 lorry acquired by Wynns in 1922 was almost certainly an ex-War Department machine.

One of nine Sentinel steam lorries operated by Wynns, this four-wheeler was acquired in 1929, having been supplied new to Spillers a year earlier.

This solid-tyred 45-ton Scammell tractor was new to G Earle of Hull, passing to Wynns in 1935.

Born in 1821 near Cullumpton in Devon, Thomas Wynn started his working life modestly enough as a contract cleaner of railway carriages in Exeter. Working on the railway took him to Paddington and then to Newport, South Wales, where he was employed by the Brunel's Great Western Railway (GWR). But, at the age of 42, something made Thomas Wynn consider his future and its possibilities. He had a rapidly growing family and faced a bleak future if he continued to work as a cleaner. Ultimately, his family would number eight daughters and just two sons. If the numbers had been stacked the other way around, perhaps Thomas might not have felt the need to take serious action. But as it was, he decided his prospects with the GWR were limited.

Working in Newport, he saw both the strengths and the weaknesses of the railway. It was excellent as a means of bringing goods in large quantities down the main line to Newport, but onward distribution presented something of a problem. Canals, packhorses and mules were the only options thereafter. And so, in 1863, Thomas Wynn purchased a couple of horses and carts and established himself as a carrier in the Newport region.

Wynns first Scammell was this solid-tyred articulated low-loader, acquired in 1927. Over the years, the products of the Watford company became increasingly important. 'HP' is driving – 'RT' stands alongside.

As well as carrying goods that had been brought to Newport by rail, Thomas soon had the good fortune to form an association with Star Flour Mills in the town. He found himself distributing flour for the Star Flour Mills to the many bakeries and shops in the valleys of South Wales, an alliance which was to continue for many decades.

Thomas died in 1878 aged 57 years. At the time of his death his company had expanded to include several dozen horses and carts... those new-fangled horseless carriages had yet to appear! The running of the business was taken on by Thomas's son, Robert, who was just 15 when his father died. Family legend has it that Robert was too small to put the collars over the heads of the shire horses and his older sister, Emma, was also enlisted to help run the business.

Within four years, at the age of 19, Robert had married Nora Small. The marriage, it seems, was fortuitous. Nora's father was Samuel Small, a prominent Newport haulier who specialised in the extraction of round timber from local forests. When Samuel Small died two years later, Robert was offered his father-in-law's business, but instead insisted that it should go to auction, where he purchased it. It was this that started Wynns' 80-year long association with the timber haulage business.

The company was becoming something of a fixture.

Alongside the existing round timber and regular haulage activities, Robert had spotted other possibilities. The steelworks at Newport were expanding rapidly and heavy haulage was on the horizon. By 1890, he had built a horse-drawn wagon which was capable of hauling what at the time was considered a staggering 40 tons in weight... with the assistance of 48 horses, harnessed in teams, four abreast! The rig was used to carry heavy machinery from the Mill Street railway sidings to the Lysaght Steel Works which had originally been established in Bristol to produce corrugated iron in 1857. These heavy haulage activities began to establish a high profile for Wynns and, over the years, became crucial to the company's success. Wynns' vehicles regularly found themselves being called upon to shift all manner of difficult loads, up to 40 tons in weight.

It was also during this decade that Robert introduced steam power into the business, employing Fowler and Garrett traction engines and tractors for loads that did not suit the horses. Continued growth of the business led to the acquisition of premises at Shaftesbury Street, Newport where there was

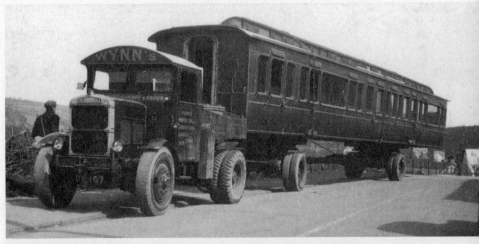

Queen Victoria's royal coach being transported from Newcastle Emlyn Station, Cardigan to Aberporth. The tractor is a 1930 Scammell which passed to Wynns in 1933 and was rebuilt for timber hauling duties.

5-ton Fowler steam locomotive bought new by Wynns in 1920 and registered the following year. The machine has survived and, following a period under the care of Newport Council, is now in private hands.

DW 2121 again, this time coupled to a flat-top solid-tyred boiler trailer, dating from 1890, which has been loaded with a 30-ton stator destined for Newport Power Station. The date is 1921.

Dating from May 1935, this Garner TW60 was one of four used on regular deliveries throughout South Wales.

Photographed in 1931, DW 7652 was one of a pair of Scammell six-wheeled 6-tonners acquired in 1931 and used for overnight deliveries to the London area.

DW 7653 was the second of the Scammell chain-driven six-wheelers.

stabling for 200 horses and accommodation for Robert, his wife and their growing family.

Like his father before him, Robert fathered ten children; though unlike his father he was lucky enough to have eight boys and two girls (two of the boys died in infancy). Eventually he was joined in the business by all but one of his sons, each of whom contributed to the firm's continued expansion. One son, Alan, became a farmer. While this may seem surprising, it is interesting to note that Robert Wynn himself entered farming for a while as a means of providing hay and weekend grazing land for the large number of horses that the business employed. At the end of work on a Saturday, all the horses were herded out to the fields until Monday morning, when they were driven back to the Shaftesbury Street premises. It must have been quite a sight.

At the outbreak of the Great War in 1914, some of the company's traction engines were commandeered by the War Office. Nevertheless, Wynns became involved in moving heavy guns and other equipment, and was also able to continue with the extraction of felled timber, going on to establish a depot at Welshpool to service this aspect of the business.

The company's first internal-combustion engined vehicle, a 25hp petrol-engined Palladium truck, was acquired in 1916. Perhaps slightly better known for its motor cars, Palladium was an obscure maker who, until about 1922, assembled trucks in Putney, south London from French components. The second such vehicle, a 59bhp Karrier, followed three years later, with a pair of rebuilt ex-WD Subsidy type solid-tyred Albions joining the fleet in 1921 and 1922.

Early in 1923, the company was incorporated as Robert Wynn & Sons Limited, with the capital shared equally between Robert and his wife, Nora. When Robert died in November of that year, his share was divided equally between his three eldest sons, Samuel, Robert Thomas – always known as 'RT' to distinguish him from his father, and George, the latter often known by his initials as 'OG'. It is a matter of Wynn family pride that, when the company was eventually sold in 1946, all five of the brothers involved in the enterprise and their families were given equal shares.

By the early 1920s, steam traction engines were being phased out and were replaced by Sentinel steam wagons... the maker, incidentally, always insisting on the spelling 'waggons'... along with a single Foden (registered DW 4040), acquired in

Chain-driven Scammell 45-ton tractor coupled to a drop-frame trailer carrying a Ruston Hornsby boiler. This tractor was a significant component of the company's early heavy haulage fleet.

March 1925. This had the distinction of being the first mechanically-propelled articulated vehicle in the country and was often driven by Percy Wynn – one of the younger of the five Wynn brothers and known to everyone as 'HP'. Percy had originally been apprenticed to the steam locomotive manufacturers John Fowler of Leeds, and had actually worked on the construction of DW 4040, and had also driven it to South Wales when it was purchased by the company.

After joining the family business in the early 1920s, on one famous occasion 'HP' drove the articulated Foden from Southampton to Cardiff with the semi-trailer loaded with a massive ship's propeller on a flat-bed semi-trailer. The 140-mile journey took four days when loaded, and three days with the wagon running empty. 'HP' was also no stranger to the cab of the Fowler 5-ton steam locomotive *Dreadnought* which had been acquired for £1,587 in August 1920... more than £50,000 at today's prices.

Wynns initiated regular runs, known as the 'London trunk', carrying tinplate to the capital from the Mellingriffith Tin Plate works at Whitchurch, Glamorgan and bringing back bacon, Chinese eggs

Front view of KH 9895 showing the width of the load. This tractor was sold during WW2 and broken up in 1963.

and tinned foodstuffs from Cross & Blackwell, as well as toffees from Sharpes, intended for wholesalers in and around Newport. Heavy cable reels were shipped all over the region from the Standard Telephones plant at Newport, and steel was carried from Lysaght's Orb Works at Newport.

Years later, at the age of 11, John used to hitch a ride to Lysaght's in one of the Scammell 'light sixes' on a Saturday morning and, once the truck was beyond the weighbridge, he was allowed by the regular driver to drive it into the works and to help rope and sheet the load before returning to the weighbridge for the outward journey. As the Jesuits used to say... get 'em young and you get 'em for life!

Further expansion saw the opening of a depot, which included a yard and stables, at Collingdon Road in Cardiff and 'RT' moved to Cardiff to run the operation.

Although the Foden already referred to had been the company's first articulated vehicle, the days of steam haulage were clearly coming to an end. Weight restrictions introduced in the 'Road Traffic Act' of 1930 reduced the useful payload below break-even and this finally brought an end to the dominance of steam lorries on the roads. A number of the old steam-powered vehicles remained in service for local tar-spraying contracts (road-laying for Cardiff City Council), with the steam from the boiler piped around the tar pot to keep the tar liquid.

The company's first heavy petrol-

Impressive line-up of four Garner TW60s and a pair of Sentinel steam wagons, the latter dating from 1934 for the London trunk routes.

Acquired in 1942, DDW 18 was a Foden DG heavy tractor for drawbar work. It was the first 100-tonner acquired by the company and one of only three produced. It was scrapped in 1958. Note the 120-ton load – clearly overloading was common practice.

engined vehicle, a solid-tyred chain-driven tractor-trailer combination from Scammell of Watford, had been acquired in 1927, as was a very interesting short-wheelbase Chevrolet drawbar tractor (DW 5608, Wynns' fleet number 67). But the Scammells prevailed, and eventually there were five petrol-engined Scammell 'super sixes' and three chain-driven Scammells. The 30-foot long six-wheelers were capable of carrying 13 tons which, at that time, was a considerable load, and were used to provide nightly long-distance trunk services between Newport, Cardiff and London, with three loaded trucks running into London each night and three empty trucks returning. After the war, the Scammells were replaced by Fodens and a lone AEC Monarch (DDW 340, Wynns' fleet number 133).

The London trunk services were considered to be sufficiently important to the business that Gordon Wynn, the fifth and youngest of the brothers, moved to London to manage operations from that end of the route. However, during this period, heavy haulage continued to provide a glamorous aspect to the business, and heavy low-loader trailers were built or acquired which allowed loads such as railway locomotives, earth-moving equipment, huge ships' propellers, and industrial plant and machinery to be moved.

In December 1935, Wynns acquired the vehicle fleet of the Pearce Haulage Company, which included a number of heavy Scammells. One of these vehicles, a 45-ton tractor (CDW 33, Wynns' fleet number 87) on pneumatic tyres, was eventually rebuilt as a

forestry tractor and gave sterling service for a couple more decades. Other Scammells acquired at this time included a 45-ton tractor which had been bought new in 1929 by G Earle. Although it ran on solid tyres, this particular vehicle became an important element of the heavy haulage fleet all through the war years and was not broken up until the early 1960s.

During the period 1938-39 there was an enormous amount of construction activity in South Wales resulting from re-armament and the dispersal of the Royal Ordnance Factories and Wynns was at the forefront of the haulage scene. Steam-generating plant for new factories included 50-ton boilers, and batteries of these were conveyed from the dockheads and manoeuvred into their final positions using a combination of skill and experience with no small measure of brute force! Electrical equipment weighing up to 100 tons was required for extensions to the electricity generating system, and steelwork for pylons was delivered to often remote mountain sites. Where metalled surfaces did not exist, sometimes the only way that such equipment could be got into place was by using caterpillar tracks or even teams of horses.

By the outbreak of war in 1939, the fleet was a mix of steam and petrol-engined vehicles... although it is worth pointing out that a number of horse-drawn vehicles, generally pulling tipper carts, also remained in service right up to the end of the 1930s, the last of these being used on contracts for Monsanto. Sentinel steam wagons worked

The 100-ton Foden did sterling service throughout WW2, being called upon to haul all kinds of oversized loads. In this case, the load is an ore-crusher; note the tracked wheels at the rear designed to allow the plant to be moved around site.

DW 18 again, this time hauling a marine boiler which had been recovered from Pembroke beach and was on its way to the Eastern Dry Dock at Newport.

alongside petrol-engined vehicles from Garner, Bedford and Scammell. The heavy chassis produced by the Watford-based Scammell company became increasingly important in Wynns' heavy haulage activities and, by this time, the fleet included chain-drive four-, six- and eight-wheeled vehicles, in rigid and articulated chassis form. Many were still wearing solid tyres at the rear since pneumatic tyre technology had yet to develop to the point where the tyres could reliably support extreme loads.

World War 2 provided plenty of opportunity for the company to demonstrate its skill with moving heavy and awkward loads as well as continuing with regular haulage and timber contracts. During this period, Wynns contributed to the war effort with materials and equipment landed at the South Wales ports being distributed across the country. Wynns' vehicles were regularly called upon to shift tanks, aircraft, engineer's equipment, machinery, landing craft, and gun barrels, and to replace heavy factory machinery which had been destroyed in enemy air raids.

Although the fleet was not getting any younger, the nation's motor industry naturally gave priority to the military services and it was difficult for

a civilian enterprise, even one with as high a profile as Wynns, to acquire new vehicles during World War 2. However, notable acquisitions during these years included a clutch of three diesel-powered ERF tractors for use with semi-trailers, two of which (CDW 909, CDW 917, Wynns' fleet numbers 101 and 103) were powered by Gardner 5LW five-cylinder diesel engines, whilst the third (CDW 910, Wynns' fleet number 102) was fitted with the six-cylinder 6LW engine. There was also a near-unique Foden DG six-wheeled heavy drawbar tractor unit (DDW 18, Wynns' fleet number 112), the first 100-ton tractor operated by Wynns, and one of only three such machines constructed.

The end of World War 2, and the subsequent availability of war-surplus Scammells, Pacifics and Diamond Ts, ushered in what many consider to be the most interesting period in the Wynns story. As time took its inevitable toll, these old warriors were frequently re-engined and rebuilt more than once in the company's own workshops, giving sterling service for another 30 years.

Wynns never had the heavy haulage market all to themselves. This photograph shows a 45-ton Scammell operated by rivals E W Rudd, hauling a huge Hackbridge transformer bound for Alcoa via Norfolk, Virginia.

Foden DDW 18 coupled to a solid-tyred swan-neck trailer carrying a transformer; a 45-ton Scammell tractor acts as a pusher. The location is Cardiff Docks.

Flashback....

A Blackwood Hodge Marion 111M dragline excavator intended for
Tarmac Limited being carried on a 16-wheeled solid-tyred swan-neck
trailer. Note the Scammell pusher tractor at the rear.

Diamonds are fore

The decade following the end of World War 2 was a time of great change in the British road haulage industry. Nationalisation of the industry had started in 1947, and some of Wynns' trunk routes were turned over to the newly-nationalised carriers. However, the company managed to largely escape the fate which befell so many of the industry's well-known names because the percentage of exempted traffic which Wynns carried meant that the heavy haulage and round-timber work was able to remain in private hands.

Within a few years Wynns, and the nationalised Pickfords, were the only companies offering heavy-haulage services, and the former quickly expanded its operations so as to be able to compete with Pickfords across the entire country.

But heavy haulage was enjoying an unprecedented boom, for there was enormous demand for heavy-haulage services during the '50s and '60s as the country started to modernise industries

Semi-aerial view shows off the extraordinary length of the Diamond T's bonnet. The truck was originally powered by a Hercules DFXE six-cylinder diesel but this was generally replaced in Wynns' workshops with a Meadows or Cummins unit.

130-ton de-asphalting tower constructed by Babcock & Wilcox for the Anglo-Iranian Oil Company and destined for the refinery at Llandarcy. The vessel is being carried on a pair of four-line flat top bogies.

This 100-ton vessel was delivered, manoeuvred into position and off-loaded for the UK Atomic Energy Authority (AEA).   *Picture: Nuclear Decommissioning Authority*

Handwritten notes on the reverse of the original of this photograph indicate that the total weight of the trailer and load is 149 tons and includes a calculation regarding the load-bearing abilities of the 15.00x20 20-ply tyres on the trailer.

In 1952, Diamond T EDW 96 hauled this propane vessel from London, where it had been built in G A Harvey's Charlton works, to the BP refinery at Llandarcy. A Jaguar belonging to 'HP' can be seen in front of the tractor.

ver

Above: With the exception of Wynns' distinctive red and black livery, this Diamond T Model 980, EDW 95, looks much as it did when it left the factory in Chicago, in 1941. One of around 23 so acquired by Wynns from 1947, it hauls a huge English Electric transformer with pusher assistance from a 45-ton Scammell through London's northern outskirts.

which had been decimated by the long years of war.

For example, the Central Electricity Authority (CEA), which had been established in 1948 and which was later to become the Central Electricity Generating Board (CEGB), struggled to build sufficient generating and distribution capacity to accommodate the increasing demand for electricity. At the same time, there was much rebuilding and expansion of the nationalised gas, coal and steel industries and, at times, it must have seemed that huge transformers, generators, fractionating columns, boilers, and stators were criss-crossing the country as the Wynns and Pickfords crews struggled to manoeuvre massive loads along the, as yet, unmodernised

Beginning to look a little the worse for wear, Diamond T FDW 533 is shown coupled to a 16-wheeled soild-tyred trailer with a high load. In the days before hydraulic suspension, the use of solid tyres reduced the overall height of the trailer and load.

British road network. Without the benefit of motorways and bypasses, it was often necessary to thread these huge pieces of equipment through the narrow streets of towns which had changed little in the previous two or three hundred years.

Bridges were also a particular problem, since safe loadings on older bridges were often little more than guesswork. In this respect, Pickfords suffered a most unfortunate accident in 1945. The company was transporting an 80-ton roll housing from Davy-United in Sheffield to Falkirk in Scotland using a Cranes solid-tyred trailer, with a Diamond T tractor at either end. The route involved crossing the River Ure on the old A1 at Boroughbridge in North Yorkshire and the second span of the 16th Century stone bridge gave way after the first tractor and the first bogie of the trailer had crossed it. As the bridge collapsed into the river, the rear bogie of the trailer fell away, taking the second tractor and the load with it, and virtually blocking the river. The crew were unharmed but a subsequent

With the pusher tractor uncoupled and the draw-bar hanging loose, Diamond T EDW 96 negotiates a chemical vessel through the streets of Swansea.

Pausing for a well-earned rest, Diamond T FDW 922 is hauling one of two 93-ton castings designed to be used as mill housings from the works of Davy-United at Sheffield to the Steel Company of Wales. The date is 1951 and the crew is led by Bryn Groves.

Coupled to Diamond T ODW 937, and riding on a pair of four-line flat-top bogies, the load is destined for one of the first-generation of Britain's nuclear power stations.

Wynns carrying three of the roll housings and Pickfords carrying the other three. After the accident happened, 'HP' rang 'RT', who was holidaying in Torquay at the time, and suggested that he made the trip to Boroughbridge – a round trip of more than 600 miles – to take a look for himself. Needless to say, 'RT' was horrified by what he saw! Perhaps it was more luck than anything else which had allowed Wynns to escape a similar fate, but the two companies were operating in a very similar manner.

The Royal Engineers erected a temporary Bailey Bridge across the river whilst the bridge was rebuilt but the incident persuaded the Ministry of Transport that a survey of the nation's bridges might not be a bad idea to prevent a similar disaster occurring elsewhere.

investigation showed that poor workmanship had been at fault when the bridge was widened in the 18th Century.

The accident could so easily have happened to a Wynns crew since both companies were contracted to carry the same loads across the same route, with

Crawling slowly up Newport's Barrack Hill, Diamond T NDW 232, together with a Diamond T pusher, struggles with a huge 80-90 ton excavator.

Re-cabbed Diamond T TDW 241, acquired by Wynns in 1959, leaves the Ferranti works with a 30kVA transformer, the largest ever supplied to the CEGB.

Both the British and US Armies had used Diamond T tractors in the tank-transporter role during World War 2 and, similarly, both Pickfords and Wynns found that the military Diamond T was an ideal heavy prime mover, which was more than capable of shifting exceptional loads.

Pickfords had been in the fortunate position of having been able to acquire six or seven Diamond T tractors brand-new during the war. Denied this opportunity, Wynns had found that such machinery was in short supply and it wasn't until the end of the war that the company had been able to acquire Diamond Ts through the surplus market. Percy 'HP' Wynn was already well aware of what the Diamond T could do... whilst following a convoy of these vehicles on the Cardiff to

From the vantage point of an upper story window, Diamond T EDW 95 can be seen negotiating an 80-ton alternator constructed by English Electric at Stafford and on its way to Fulham Power Station, London.

Diamond T HDW 107 hauling an electric locomotive constructed by British Thomson Houston (BTH) on a pneumatic-tyred low-loader trailer.

Like several of the Wynns' Diamond T's, PDW 321 was re-cabbed but it is arguable whether the new cabs, constructed in Wynns' workshops, equalled the splendour of the original 'art deco' Diamond T units.

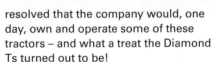

Newport road, he had been hugely impressed when one of the convoy was forced to brake hard. The air-assisted braking system allowed the truck to lock-up all eight rear wheels, leaving tyre tracks along the road. This was a feat which no contemporary British truck could match. He was apparently so impressed that when he returned to the depot he insisted that John and his father, 'OG', come back with him to take a look at the black tracks in the road, which were still clearly visible. 'HP'

resolved that the company would, one day, own and operate some of these tractors – and what a treat the Diamond Ts turned out to be!

The Diamond T Model 980, and the later Model 981, was the result of a British Purchasing Commission requirement for a ballast-bodied draw-bar tractor which could supplement the Scammell Pioneer 30-ton tank transporter. Although competent enough, the ageing Scammell was never available in sufficient numbers and lacked the capacity to handle the ever-increasing weight of tanks being introduced into service during World War 2.

The project kicked-off in late 1940, when the British Purchasing Commission approached several American manufacturers of heavy trucks with a specification for a 40-ton diesel-engined tractor. One of the prime considerations was that the chosen vehicle could be put into production immediately and, of the manufacturers approached, it was the Chicago-based Diamond T company that was eventually chosen.

The vehicle which they produced was described as the Model 980 (the 981 differed only in having winch fairlead rollers at the front), and was derived from their civilian 12-ton Model 512. In common with many US manufacturers of heavy trucks, Diamond T did not build engines and a Hercules DFXE six-cylinder diesel unit was chosen to power the Model 980, producing around 200bhp from its 14.5 litres. The transmission was a four-

Technical specification
Diamond T Models 980, 981

Identification
Manufacturer: Diamond T Motor Car Company; Chicago, Illinois.

Manufacturer's designation: Model 980, Model 981.

Production: 1941-45.

Number produced: 6,500 approximately.

Number in service with Wynns: 30.

Specification
Engine: Hercules DFXE; six cylinders in-line; diesel; water-cooled; 14,500cc; overhead valves; power output, 201bhp at 1,800rpm; maximum torque, 684 lbf/ft. A number were subsequently fitted with Meadows 6DC.970 diesel engines and then with Cummins units.

Transmission: 4F1Rx2.

Drive line: 6x4.

Suspension: live axles on multi-leaf semi-elliptical springs.

Brakes: air pressure.

Electrical system: hybrid 6V/12V/24V.

Dimensions (as built)
Length, 360in; **width,** 114in; **height,** 62in.

Wheelbase: 179in.

Bogie centres: 52in.

Weight: unladen, 26,712 lb; authorised gross train weight, 178,079 lb.

Performance: maximum speed, 23mph.

speed unit, in combination with a two-speed transfer box. Whilst the choice of a diesel unit provided commonality with the Gardner-powered Scammell already being operated by the British Army, and was positively welcomed by both Wynns and Pickfords after the war, diesel was not the favoured fuel of the US Army, which tended to prefer petrol, and the Diamond T was one of only a very few diesel-powered trucks in the US Army and, largely because of the diesel engine was classified as 'substitute standard'. The US Army referred to the tractor as the M20, and described the tank-transporter train, including the 40/45-ton trailer, as M19.

Delivery of the first Diamond T tractors was scheduled for 1941, and the truck remained in production until 1945, by which time around 6,500 of these superb vehicles had been produced. A total of 2,255 were used by the British Army... and more than a few were certainly lost beneath the Atlantic as a result of enemy attacks on the convoy routes. Despite often being called upon to perform under the most difficult conditions, the truck was described by the military as being 'most reliable' and many believe that the Diamond T, with its stylish 'art deco' cab and outrageous V-shaped windscreen, was the best looking truck of World War 2. Sadly, in August 1943, the civilian cab was replaced by a standard military-style open cab that

Equipped with a fifth wheel for use with low-loader semi-trailer number 334, HDW 107 is parked-up for the night. The load weighs 64 tons.

Picture: Nuclear Decommissioning Authority

did little to improve the truck's appearance, but otherwise there were few changes.

The standard trailer for transporting tanks was a multi-axle 40-45-ton design manufactured by Cranes, Dyson and a number of other companies in Britain, with similar designs produced by Rogers, Fruehauf, Winter-Weiss, and Pointer-Williamette in the USA. There were also experiments with adapting the Diamond T for use with a semi-trailer.

With the war finally out of the way, Diamond Ts started to appear on the

surplus market, and the first two were acquired by Wynns in 1947. With the civilian registration numbers EDW 95 and EDW 96 (Wynns' fleet numbers 160 and 161), these two trucks were the first of a total of 30 of these splendid machines that were eventually acquired, along with a number of the matching trailers. With their economical... well, relatively economical... diesel engines, Wynns were able to put the Diamond Ts to work straight away. Notwithstanding some self-inflicted problems with cylinder-head gaskets, the trucks

EDW 95 was the first Diamond T to be put into service with Wynns, dating from May 1947. Here she receives assistance from a Scammell at the rear. The winch fairlead rollers in the front bumper reveal that EDW 95 is the rarer Model 981.

Extreme loads place considerable stresses on bridges, here EDW 95 keeps to the very centre of the spans.

proved to be very reliable. Back then, anti-freeze was an expensive commodity and the capacity of the cooling system of a Diamond T was 61 US quarts! To save money, the crews were told to either drain the cooling systems at night or to use a paraffin heater under the sump to avoid freezing. Of course, if a truck had returned to the yard after a hard day's work then the engine should have been allowed to cool down before it was drained, but this wasn't always done and the result was that the cylinder heads would become distorted leading to gasket failure.

All of the tractors were continuously modified and rebuilt in the company's own workshops to suit their hard-working life, some eventually receiving new cabs as well as Meadows and then Cummins engines in place of the Hercules diesel.

The draw-bar configuration proved to be extremely versatile and the vehicles were used, both solo and in tandem, with a whole range of special trailers, and at least two (HDW 107, fleet number 199 and RDW 976, fleet number 281) had the big steel ballast body removed, to be converted to fifth-wheel form.

A pair of Diamond Ts acting in tandem was a fine sight, and between them the tractors were more than capable of shifting loads up to 130 tons. These tractors formed the mainstay of the Wynns heavy-haulage fleet for around 25 years, moving all manner of over-sized and over-weight loads. Even when they were withdrawn from regular service they remained useful – Bryn Lavender, Wynns' number one welder, cut up two Diamond Ts and used the rear axles and parts of the chassis to make the steerable bogies that carried the concrete beams being used to construct the Coldra Viaduct on the M4.

More than one ex-Wynns' Diamond T has survived into preservation. •

A pair of Diamond Ts, the rear tractor clearly working hard, struggle to negotiate a heavy transformer along the Pontypool to Ystrad Mynach road, *en route* to the Crumlin substation.

Those magnificent Pacifics

With assistance from a Diamond T at the rear, *Dreadnought* brings a huge English Electric transformer through Birmingham city centre.

I n 1950, Wynns' Diamond Ts were eclipsed by another ex-military vehicle... the incredible Pacific TR1 – or M26 to use the military designation. With its armoured cab, massive 17.5-litre Hall-Scott petrol engine, three-speed transfer box and huge chain-driven bogie, the Pacific was probably the largest and most powerful truck in the world at the time. Uncompromising in its appearance and construction, it was dubbed the 'Dragon Wagon' by its US Army crews.

When Japan's attack on Pearl Harbor encouraged the USA to join the war in 1941, the only heavy tank transporter available to the US Army was the Diamond T but the US

The soft-skin variant of the Pacific, designated M26A1, was considerably lighter than its armoured predecessor.

It was this North British railway locomotive load, destined for the Festival of Britain on London's South Bank, that really put Wynns on the heavy-haulage map. Hauled by Pacific *Dreadnought*, the 105-ton locomotive was brought to the site on a swan-neck frame using special girders, carried on solid-tyred bogies... and was removed on the brand-new Cranes pneumatic-tyred trailer with hydraulic steering and suspension.

Army was unhappy with the vehicle for a number of reasons. Firstly, it was diesel powered and no comparable US trucks at the time were fitted with diesel engines. They would also have preferred a fifth-wheel machine with a higher rating to accommodate the increasingly-heavy tanks coming out of the tank arsenals. It was also unarmoured and so was not suitable for operation in combat areas... and lastly, it was in short supply.

For these reasons, the US Army started looking for an alternative tractor-trailer combination for the transportation and recovery of tanks, on and off the battlefield.

One vehicle that was considered for possible evaluation was a huge forward-control tractor that had been produced by the Knuckey Truck Company of San Francisco especially for this application. Knuckey had been established in 1943 in response to a shortage of manufacturers of heavy custom-built trucks on the West Coast and specialised in heavy-duty off-road machines for use in open-cast mining and quarrying applications. The company's speciality was a patented centre-pivot double roller chain drive system. Designated TR1, Knuckey's proposal for the Army's tank-transporter requirement was based on the chassis of an existing Knuckey truck, and was powered by a Hall-Scott 400 engine, a monstrous six-cylinder petrol unit producing 240bhp from its more than 17.5 litres... and with some 800 lbf/ft of torque available. This power unit, which had been introduced by Hall Scott in 1940, and was described as 'the most-powerful truck engine built', was coupled to the patented Knuckey centre-pivoted walking-beam rear bogie via a four-speed Fuller gearbox and three-speed transfer case, with final drive by massive triple roller chains. The un-braked front axle was suspended on semi-elliptical springs, whilst at the rear the walking beam was unsprung. The maximum road speed – without load – was 26mph and the truck was enormously thirsty, consuming

Jostling for space with the regular traffic, including three or four other ex-military vehicles, Pacific *Dreadnought* hauls a beam-suspended Ferranti transformer on a pair of pneumatic-tyred bogies.

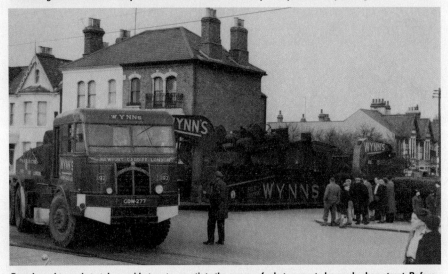

Dreadnought needs to take a wide turn to negotiate the corner of what seems to be a suburban street. Before the advent of the motorways and bypasses, the only way of moving these massive loads was through town and city streets.

With a Diamond T at the rear, Pacific *Dreadnought* negotiates a huge casting for a steel crucible through the factory gates where it has been constructed.

fuel at a rate of just 1.08 miles per gallon.

With its brutally angular armoured forward-control cab, featuring hinged shutters for the windscreen and side windows, the truck would have won no prizes in a beauty competition but, my goodness, it more than made up for this with presence!

Unlike the ballast-bodied Diamond T, the truck was fitted with a fifth-wheel, and was designed to be coupled to a purpose-designed 45-ton semi-trailer produced by Fruehauf. The semi-trailer was fitted with folding loading ramps at the rear, and also had two pairs of hinged ramps which were folded across the large rear bogie to allow the load to pass over the wheels. Early production examples lacked these hinged ramps but, instead, featured twin wheels on either side of the trailer that could be moved closer together or further apart to accommodate different widths of armoured fighting vehicle. There were two huge winches fitted behind the cab of the tractor to assist with loading disabled tanks, and a folding 'A' frame that enabled the truck to act as a recovery vehicle.

Knuckey was too small to undertake the volume of production required by the US Army and production was entrusted to the Pacific Car & Foundry Company of West Seattle in Washington state, a manufacturer of railway locomotives and wagons in peacetime. Knuckey's involvement in the project continued through the supply of the massive rear bogies.

Between 1943 and 1944, some 1,372 of these monster machines were produced and, when the armoured version was replaced by a soft-skin variant in 1944, a further 800 or so were constructed. Shipped as deck cargo to Britain during the last years of the war, the trucks were used almost exclusively by the US Army and saw service in Normandy, as well as being used widely during the advance across Europe.

The machine first came to the attention of 'HP' when one of the Wynns' crews told him how they had been parked in a lay-by waiting for a police escort when a US Army tank-transporter convoy, consisting of four Pacifics complete with semi-trailers and loaded with Sherman tanks, pulled into the lay-by, parking on the grass verge whilst the crews went into the nearby cafe for a cup of coffee. The Wynns' crew allowed themselves a small degree of professional amusement as they saw that the weight of the outfits had caused them to sink into the soft ground. However, their amusement turned to astonishment when the US Army crews returned, climbed into the cabs and simply pulled away, the outfits

The crew pose beside a Pacific tractor, together with a swan-necked trailer on two three-line pneumatic-tyred bogies, prior to entering the British Thomson Houston works at Rugby to pick up a load.

At a time when the standard maximum width for trucks was 90in, the 150in width of the Pacific tractors often meant a very tight fit through narrow streets...

... and around tight bends! Trailer 333 was the first hydraulically-steered and suspended unit in service.

having no trouble at all in extricating themselves from the deeply-rutted ground.

Inevitably, the end of the war meant that some of the tractors never left these shores and, in 1950, Percy Wynn learned that a number were available for sale... from a quarry in Kent! He purchased six at a cost of £400 each,

swiftly followed by four more for parts. Wynns had little need of the heavy armoured cabs, and something like a ton-and-a-half of high-grade steel was stripped off each of the trucks in the company's workshops, and Percy was pleased to be able to recover much of the cost of purchase by selling the steel for scrap.

It was Percy's intention that these huge tractors would be able to handle over-sized loads which were too big even for the Diamond Ts, but as the six Pacifics gradually entered service... a process which, incidentally, took almost 15 years... they bore little resemblance to the uncompromisingly-military machines which had been turned out of

Resplendent with its new cab and shining black and red livery, Pacific *Dreadnought* brings a 15kVA transformer from the GEC works, bound for Uskmouth. The transformer is suspended in a pair of beams carried on the bogies of trailer 333.

Photographed in 1957, *Helpmate* carries a large, beam-suspended, transformer to Cardiff Docks. The tractor entered service with Wynns in 1951 and ended up being sold in Cyprus following a contract on the island. Two Diamond Ts are bringing up the rear.

Technical specification
Pacific TR1

Identification

Manufacturer: Pacific Car & Foundry Company; Renton, Seattle.

Manufacturer's designation: TR1.

Production: 1943-45.

Number produced:
2,172 approximately.

Number in service with Wynns: 6.

Specification

Engine (as manufactured): Hall Scott Model 440; six cylinders in-line; petrol; water-cooled; 17,861cc; overhead valves; power output, 240bhp at 2100rpm; maximum torque, 800 lbf/ft. Re-engined by Wynns using Hercules DFXE engines taken from Diamond Ts, and by turbo-charged Cummins units.

Transmission: 4F1Rx3.

Drive line: part-time 6x6.

Suspension: live front axle on multi-leaf semi-elliptical springs; walking-beam rear bogie without suspension.

Brakes: air pressure, rear wheels only.

Electrical system: 12V.

Dimensions (as built)

Length, 304in; **width,** 150in; **height,** 137in.

Wheelbase: 172in.

Bogie centres, 63in.

Weight: unladen, 42,000 lb; authorised gross train weight – 133,000-143,000 lb.

Performance: maximum speed, 26mph.

A pair of Pacifics, headed by *Valiant*, photographed with a Ruston Bucyrus 11-RB dragline excavator on a swan-neck trailer carried on a pair of four-line bogies. The trailer, 456, ended up in the Sudan via Hardwick's yard, Ewell.

Pacific's railway works in Renton, Washington half a decade or so earlier.

The high fuel consumption was the most serious disadvantage and the remedy lay in replacing the thirsty Hall-Scott engines with a more economical diesel unit. The trucks were rebuilt in Wynns' workshops as they were required for service, with the petrol engines initially ousted in favour of Hercules DFXE engines taken from Diamond Ts and latterly, turbo-charged Cummins units. At the same time, the manual Fuller gearboxes were replaced by semi-automatic units, which gave easier gear changes and reduced the shock loading on the driveline... and the Pacific was also the first of the Wynns' vehicles to feature power steering! We have come to take power steering for granted, even on modest motor cars, but back then no commercial trucks featured such luxury... even the Diamond T lacked such a facility and the driver was presented with a huge ` 22-inch steering wheel in an attempt to reduce the effort involved in heaving the beast around corners.

The military fifth wheel was removed and replaced by a small ballast body, allowing the trucks to be used with draw-bar trailers, and the cabs were also rebuilt. On some tractors, the original military wheels were comprehensively reinforced, presumably as a result of experience... but the distinctive triple-roller chain drive, with its total loss lubrication system that left a trail of oil wherever the trucks were driven, remained.

Pushing, rather than pulling, Pacific *Helpmate* is coupled to a 150-ton 275kVA transformer built by British Thomson Houston at Rugby. In 1953, this was the heaviest single piece of electrical equipment to be moved on British roads.

With additional castor wheels under the swan necks, trailer 666 was rated at 200 tons. Here the trailer, loaded with a mill casting from Davy-United, is being pulled by a Pacific tractor and pushed by a pair of Diamond Ts.

Watched by its crew and by a small crowd, *Dreadnought* carefully negotiates a transformer under a low bridge at Pipe Gate, Shropshire.

John Wynn, who would have been just 18 or so when the first Pacific entered service in late 1950, took it on himself to name the tractors, selecting the names *Dreadnought* (Wynns' fleet number 192, GDW 277), *Helpmate* (196, GDW 585), *Conqueror* (193, HDW 122), *Challenger* (195, YDW 356), *Valiant* (194, 1570 DW) and *Enterprise* (197, ADW 228B). The last named, which has survived into preservation in the ownership of Mike Lawrence, did not enter service until December 1964.

The first load to be associated with these monsters – perhaps the most eye-catching one – was a 105-ton North British locomotive intended for the Indian State Railways. Pickfords already had a contract to transport 100 of these locomotives from the North British works at Springburn, Glasgow to the docks, and believed that they would, almost by right, also be asked to move one locomotive to London for the Festival of Britain. However, Wynns were lighter on their feet and, without the beams necessary to actually undertake the project, Percy Wynn was able to effectively take the contract to deliver this locomotive to London from under state-controlled Pickford's nose. Only once he had the contract in the bag did he order the steel beams that were required to construct the trailer, persuading Fairfields of Chepstow to design and construct a pair of special 45-foot long beams which included provision for cross girders which could support a length of railway track, a task which took just two months! Fairfields had previously worked with Wynns over a ten-year period, producing the necks and girders for the three 'Navy' trailers (Wynns' fleet numbers 301, 302, 303) as well as a complete riveted 80-ton fixed double swan-neck trailer (Wynns' fleet number 300).

The ends of the special beams were constructed so that they could sit in the base of the swan necks of trailer 303. In April 1951, using the beams and the swan necks, the locomotive was delivered to the Festival of Britain site on London's South Bank from the Surrey Docks, where it had been brought by ship from Glasgow. The coal and water tender was moved separately by one of Wynns' Diamond Ts. When the Festival closed and the locomotive left for the docks in September, for onward transportation to India, the beams had been modified to fit into the swan necks of a brand-new trailer and one that was a first for Wynns... a 150-ton Cranes 16-wheel unit with large pneumatic tyres, and hydraulic suspension and steering. This trailer, numbered 333 in the Wynns' fleet, signalled a change in technique for the crews as the rear tractor in a push-pull

Helpmate hauls a 100-ton excavator base through the streets of Coventry. The trailer, 555, was rated for 150 tons.

Dreadnought carries a heavy transformer destined for Uskmouth Power Station; note how the transformer is suspended in a pair of beams which are, in turn, carried on hydraulically-steered and suspended bogies.

Heavy castings being delivered to Richard Thomas & Baldwin's Spencer Works at Llanwern; *Helpmate* pulls whilst a Diamond T pushes.

configuration was now required only for its additional power; steering inputs for the rear bogie of the trailer were now provided by the trailer's own hydraulic system.

This was the load that really put Wynns on the heavy haulage map.

However, the largest and heaviest piece of equipment shifted by these incredible machines were six 220-ton transformers which were transported from the English Electric factory at Stafford to Ferrybridge Power Station in Yorkshire in about 1967. No less than

three of the Pacific tractors were required for the first move, and a subsequent lift saw four of the tractors move a 212-ton 400kV Ferranti transformer across the Pennines... the steepest section of which took some three hours. The transformers were

Here, a Pacific tractor is being aided by the Foden DW 118 to negotiate this 130-ton de-asphalting tower at Llandarcy Refinery.

Pacific *Conqueror*, aided by a pair of Diamond Ts, hauls a heavy casting on a Cranes trailer.

Coupled to a swan-neck trailer riding on two three-line bogies, and with a Diamond T at the rear, *Helpmate* hauls a 120-ton stator destined for Uskmouth Power Station.

carried on a special 48-wheeled air-lift equipment (ALE) trailer – often described as a 'hover' trailer – which had been developed by Rex Farrell of the CEGB to reduce axle loadings, and thus avoid large sums of money being spent on rebuilding bridges when exceptionally heavy loads had to be moved across weak bridges.

Three of Wynns' standard trailers, numbers 789, 987 and 999, as well as two Pickfords' trailers were adapted to work with the blower equipment, which was carried in a separate Commer truck. Four B81 eight-cylinder Rolls-Royce engines were installed in the back of the truck to drive the fans, and large diameter circular ducts conveyed the high-pressure air to the load-

carrying trailers. A later variation of this equipment was self-contained and did not require the separate truck to house the blowers.

Powerful, distinctive and always immaculately turned-out, the Pacifics became something of a legend over the years and it seems that no-one was immune to the charisma of these mighty machines, even if some chose to show their appreciation in a different way. 'RT' Wynn was a case in point. When a lack of space at Newport meant that a Pacific had to be stored at the Cardiff yard 'RT' was amazed at the sheer size of the thing and when he discovered that one Pacific could haul an M1A1 heavy wrecker up the hill into a steelworks where it had previously

required two Diamond Ts, he took to referring to the Pacific as the 'Austin 7'!

For some two decades the Pacifics, and the older Diamond Ts, formed the backbone of Wynns' heavy-haulage fleet, with several of the former remaining in service way past Wynns' centenary celebrations in 1963…. even into the 1970s. But the age of the ex-military tractor started to come to an end in 1966 when Wynns, by that time part of United Transport, took delivery of the first of 25 new Scammell Contractors. Initially rated at 100 tons but subsequently up-rated to 150 and then 240 tons, these machines proved themselves to be more than worthy successors to the Pacifics and Diamond Ts.   •

Pacific *Enterprise* has survived into preservation. Restored by owner Mike Lawrence, who bought the beast more than 20 years ago, it is a common sight at various steam rallies across the south-west.

Flashback...

Diamond T tractor number 165, acquired in July 1948, coupled to the 40/45-ton tank transporter trailer for which it was originally designed. The load is a large boiler.

Old soldiers never die

Although popular with rivals Pickfords, Wynns operated just three of the ex-WD Scammell Pioneer tank transporters. This example has been heavily modified at the front end.

During World War 2, the USA became known as 'the arsenal of democracy' and, as well as producing literally hundreds of thousands of guns and tanks, produced more than three million soft-skin transport vehicles.

Under the provisions of the Lend-Lease Act of 1941, vehicles and equipment worth more than $42 billion were supplied to more than 44 countries, with many of the vehicles used by the British coming directly from the USA.

At the end of the war thousands of military vehicles remained in Britain and Europe, surplus to requirements and destined for disposal... the US manufacturers having wisely insisted that surplus vehicles were not repatriated. The British Government kept thousands for the post-war reconstruction of the British Army, but also elected to sell surplus vehicles to other nations. At the same time, many were also made available to civilians and, although some were combat-weary veterans fit only for the scrapheap, there were also unissued low-mileage examples... and all were available at a fraction of their original cost.

Wynns had received some new

vehicles during the war under government licence, allowing them to continue with vital haulage work but new civilian trucks were in short supply and remained so after the war. Like many faced with such shortages, Wynns were not alone in acquiring military-surplus vehicles, adapting them as

required for their new role... the company even purchased a pair of Jeeps as support vehicles, one in 1948, the other as late as 1961! It could be argued that ex-military vehicles effectively kept the company in business during that uneasy transition into peace which came after 1945.

Acquired in 1964, this Iron Fairy partly obscures an ex-WD Thornycroft Amazon crane, one of three such units in service with Wynns.

Indeed, the charismatic Diamond T and Pacific tractors formed the backbone of Wynns heavy-haulage fleet for the two decades following the end of World War 2.

Although the Diamond Ts and the Pacifics should be considered amongst the most significant vehicles operated by the company, they were not the only ex-military vehicles which Wynns acquired. The more mundane old warriors such as AECs, Thornycrofts, Chevrolets and Scammells might have lacked the glamour of their larger cousins, but were equally able to earn their keep at a variety of tasks.

Many of these military trucks were superb machines... simple, rugged and reliable, and built to take abuse. What they lacked in sophistication or looks they more than made up in performance and value for money. For example, in 1958, Wynns paid just £680 for a Pacific tractor at auction and £700 for a Diamond T and, over a period of 20 years or so, Percy Wynn – and, subsequently, John Wynn – purchased and operated almost 100 ex-military vehicles. Most came direct from Ministry sales but a handful had already been in civilian hands before being acquired by Wynns.

Other notable vehicles which appeared in the fleet included the AEC Matador, Chevrolet Canadian Military Pattern (CMP), Foden DG4/6, FWD SU, Scammell Pioneer, Thornycroft Amazon and Nubian, the Ward LaFrance M1A1 heavy wrecker... and, of course, the mighty Pacific. There was also a lone Federal 606 7½-ton recovery vehicle, the couple of Jeeps already referred to, a Guy FBAX, and a pair of Karrier K6s, one of these latter vehicles was the first so-called 'tackle wagon'. A Bedford QL tanker was also acquired and used as a static yard tanker.

John, himself, drove a blue-painted ex-US Navy Dodge WC54 4x4 ambulance many hundreds of miles after he reached the age of 17. Following its discharge from the services, the Dodge had already been owned by a Caernarvon farmer before he passed it to Wynns in 1949, when it was described as a 'van' on the company fleet list (Wynns' fleet number 20, JC 795). In those distant days before every household had a telephone, and before mobile phones had even been thought of, every Sunday evening, once the work schedules for the following week had been sorted out by either 'HP' or Gordon, John drove around Newport delivering notes to the drivers giving them start times and telling them whether an overnight bag might be required. Some of the responses he received are best imagined!

However, it is almost certainly true

The Ford tractor is not ex-military but it is coupled to one of the so-called Queen Mary trailers, designed for the RAF during WW2 for carrying aircraft fuselage... exactly the use to which it is being put!

The US Army's M1A1 heavy wrecker was built by both Ward LaFrance and Kenworth to a near identical design. Wynns operated seven of the splendid machines, often requiring them to double as prime movers.

to say that without these ex-military vehicles, Wynns – and many other haulage companies – would not have been able to survive the immediate post-war years.

AEC Matador O853

The AEC Matador is one of those trucks that seems to have been able to do anything that was thrown at it... it was designed by Hardy Motors in the early 1930s and was used by the British Army as a medium artillery tractor, a role which it performed admirably throughout World War 2 and into the post-war years... in fact it was so good that there was also a post-war version intended to supplement the artillery

Constructed as a medium gun tractor, the AEC Matador was one of the best British trucks of WW2 and was favoured by Wynns, who had a fleet of a dozen of them, as timber tractors and as tackle wagons.

tractor fleet whilst problems with the new Leyland Martian were resolved. It even saw some military service as a makeshift tank transporter and recovery vehicle. Early examples were petrol-engined, but most were powered by AEC's superb A173 diesel engine, a six-cylinder 7.58-litre unit driving all four wheels through a four-speed gearbox and two-speed transfer case.

The Matador was the first all-wheel drive truck to be produced in Britain in quantity and, in civilian hands during the post-war years, it found ready employment as fairground and circus transport, as a bus recovery vehicle, and as a forestry tractor where its high ground clearance, short wheelbase and forward-control cab made it ideal for working in amongst standing trees. Some Matadors even survive in this role to this day.

Wynns acquired and operated a dozen ex-military Matadors over a 13-year period, the last dating from 1971. Like many involved in the round timber trade, Wynns had favoured them as timber tractors but latterly, a number were used as tackle wagons. One, registered 1443 DW (Wynns' fleet number 115) was used by Ern Adams, the company's number one gang foreman, and was famously used to help position the huge 15in naval guns which, to this day, grace the entrance to the Imperial War Museum (IWM) at Lambeth in London. The 15in was one of the most successful British naval gun designs and was first introduced with the Queen Elizabeth Class dreadnoughts of 1915, as well as equipping the Royal Sovereign Class, and the battle cruisers HMS *Repulse*, *Renown* and *Hood*. Two similar guns, dubbed 'Clem' and 'Jane', had been

With its short wheelbase and on-board winch, the forward-control FWD SU made an ideal timber tractor.

installed as part of a shore battery near Wanstone Farm in Kent in the 1940s. 'Jane' was named after the young lady in the strip cartoon in the *Daily Mirror*, whilst 'Clem' was probably named after Winston Churchill's wife, Clementine. The IWM weapons were removed from HMS *Ramillies* (left gun) and HMS *Resolution* (right gun) and were subsequently saved from the scapyard at the last minute by the then curator of the museum who called Wynns to ask if the move was possible. John Wynn took the call and sorted out everything that was required for the job.

Chevrolet CMP

The so-called Canadian Military Pattern (CMP) vehicles were probably the most successful example of standardised vehicles from the war years. Constructed to a common pattern by both Ford and General Motors (Chevrolet) of Canada, most were of the 3-ton 4x4 configuration but the range covered a range of chassis types with the smallest being an 8cwt 4x4 and the largest, a 3-ton 6x6. The trucks

were powered either by Chevrolet's 3.5-litre six-cylinder petrol engine, or the 3.9-litre side-valve V8 Ford, and common cabs were used, making it difficult to differentiate between the products of the two manufacturers. By the end of the war Canada had produced 815,729 soft-skin vehicles, the majority of which were of the CMP type.

With its short overhangs and forward-control driving position, Wynns found that the 3-ton 4x4 could be converted into a useful timber tractor, with a pole trailer carried on a fifth wheel bolted across the shortened chassis. From 1949, ten such vehicles were acquired and put to work rated at 5 tons.

FWD SU

Alongside the heavy-haulage and regular freight business, Wynns remained very much involved in the timber trade until 1965, claiming that they were handling an average of more than a million cubic feet every year.

Scammell tractors had been used in

With the original US Army open cab replaced, Ward LaFrance wrecker EDW 340 was John Wynn's favourite truck and was kept at the Shaftesbury Street yard, ready for emergency recovery work on the local roads.

It required three Wynns' tractors to haul this 130-ton de-asphalting tower into its final position at Llandarcy Refinery – here, the Ward LaFrance M1A1 FDW 216 is coupled to the Foden DDW 18 and the Pacific *Dreadnought*.

this context before the war but the company started buying FWD CU and SU forward-control (cab over engine, or COE, in US parlance) trucks in about 1950. The American FWD company had supplied several versions of this 5-6 ton 4x4 tractor, principally under Lend-Lease, to the British Army in 1942. The Cummins diesel-powered CU was originally equipped as a timber tractor for the military, and was fitted with a powerful Gar Wood winch behind the cab; the SU was bodied as a cargo vehicle, auger drill and artillery tractor, and was powered by a Waukesha engine. There was also a tractor version for semi-trailer, and all of the variants featured permanent four-wheel drive.

Wynns purchased ten examples of either the winch-equipped artillery tractor or, possibly, the more-numerous cargo-bodied variant, removing the steel cargo bodies and equipping the

chassis either with a simple folding-jib crane for timber extraction, or as a tractor for use with a pole trailer. With its short wheelbase and forward control cab providing excellent visibility and manoeuvrability, the SU proved itself ideal for this application, and the all-wheel drive also helped to provide additional traction on muddy or steep forest tracks.

Scammell Pioneer

The heavy-duty trucks produced by the Watford-based Scammell company had always been important to the Wynns heavy-haulage operations. The first had been acquired back in 1928 and Wynns continued to buy Scammell trucks right up to the demise of that company in July 1988.

During the war, Scammell had produced thousands of their Pioneer 6x4 chassis for use as artillery tractors,

recovery vehicles and tank transporters. Originally introduced in 1928/29, the Pioneer was the first truck to incorporate Oliver North's innovative walking-beam gear case and centrally-pivoted front axle which gave it such a formidable off-road performance. Perhaps more important, from Wynns' point of view, was the low, low gearing which enabled the driver to literally inch the vehicle along in the first of its six speeds with the Gardner 6LW engine running at little more than tick-over... there was no auxiliary 'box but there was no need... the overall gearing in first was 181:1!

When surplus Pioneer tank transporters came up for sale in 1946/47, Wynns purchased two of these to supplement the pre-war Scammells which were beginning to show their age, together with one example of the recovery tractor.

The army had used the Pioneer tank transporter with a purpose-designed 30-ton semi-trailer, attached to the tractor by means of a semi-permanent sprung coupling, but Wynns chose to remove the fifth wheel, constructing a simple ballast and equipment box behind the original crew cab. With the addition of a heavy-duty tow hitch, the old Pioneer could haul an ex-military 40/45-ton multi-wheeled draw-bar trailer... the very type of trailer that had been designed for use with the Diamond T, and which was constructed by a number of British companies, including Cranes, Dyson, British Trailer Company, Hands, Shelvoke & Drury and SMT.

The trucks were reliable, if a little antiquated, but there were no further purchases, almost certainly because the Pioneers did not compare favourably to the Diamond Ts and Pacifics which became available later, and which started to appear in the fleet from 1950.

Canadian Military Pattern (CMP) vehicles were produced throughout the war by both Ford and Chevrolet of Canada. Now preserved, this example was converted for use as a timber tractor.

Scammell Pioneer tractor coupled to an ex-military 40-ton trailer loaded with a boiler. In its original tank transporter application, these tractors were used with Scammell semi-trailers.

Thornycroft Nubian

Rated by the British Army at a modest 3 tons, the wooden-bodied Thornycroft Nubian TF/AC4/1 cargo truck was typical of British logistical vehicles of World War 2 and the company produced around 5,000 of these petrol-engined all-wheel drive trucks between 1940 and 1945. Eight ex-Ministry Nubians were acquired by Wynns between 1956 and 1961; most were used as tackle wagons but at least one (Wynns' fleet number 148, DUH 701), acquired in 1961, was equipped as a timber tractor.

Thornycroft Amazon with Coles crane

Originally purchased by the RAF, the Thornycroft Amazon WF/AC6/1 carried a useful Coles electro-magnetic crane mounted on a turntable. The hoisting, slewing and derricking actions were motor driven via a direct-current generator, and automatic electro-magnetic brakes were provided to control these functions. The generator itself was driven

from a power take-off on the main gearbox. The crane could operate through 360°, and was rated to lift 5 tons at a seven foot radius.

Three of these useful vehicles were added to the fleet, the first in 1950, with the second and third examples following in 1957 and 1960. The only downside was that the petrol engine was a mite thirsty but since they were only used for general lifting and recovery work this was not a serious problem.

Ward LaFrance/Kenworth M1A1 heavy wrecker

Another of the heavy US Army trucks which saw service with Wynns was the so-called 'M1A1 heavy wrecker'. Introduced in 1943 and constructed in identical form by both Kenworth and Ward LaFrance, the M1A1 was the US Army's standard heavy recovery vehicle. It was a massive machine, equipped with a Gar Wood 5-ton swinging boom crane, a 17½-ton rear winch and a ten-ton front winch, and with a huge triangular-section front bumper ideal for pushing disabled vehicles. With its no-nonsense military

Battered, but no doubt hard-worked, Ward LaFrance M1A1 heavy wrecker about to render assistance to a Wynns' Diamond T.

appearance and open cab, the truck was unlikely to win any beauty contest prizes but the boys in Wynns' workshop fitted a new enclosed cab, constructed a useful equipment body at the rear, and welded a large open-jawed coupling on the front bumper.

In its original form, the truck was powered by a Continental 22R six-cylinder petrol engine producing 122bhp from its 8.2 litres and arranged to drive all three axles via a five-speed gearbox and two-speed transfer case; the front axle could be disengaged when not required. But, in an attempt to improve what was seriously scary fuel consumption Wynns fitted either a Gardner 5LW or 6LW diesel engine in place of the original and, whilst the maximum speed with the petrol engine had been 45mph, this was almost certainly not improved by the use of a Gardner. However, 45mph was more than adequate at a time when heavy trucks were restricted to 20mph on British roads.

In all, Wynns purchased seven of these trucks, finding them ideal for recovery work, or acting as an additional pusher, or even as the lead tractor, in a convoy when the going got tough.

During 1960, one was frequently used at the huge steel plant being

Thornycroft Amazon mobile crane engaged in a spot of heavy recovery work near Usk.

During 1960, one of Wynns' Ward LaFrance wreckers was frequently used at the huge steel plant being constructed by Richard Thomas & Baldwins on the outskirts of Newport.

constructed by Richard Thomas & Baldwins on the outskirts of Newport. When it opened in 1962 as the Spencer Works, Llanwern, it was the first oxygen-blown integrated steelworks in Britain. During construction, the low level of the land necessitated the import of thousands of tons of shale and a huge number of tippers were running to and from the site 24 hours a day. Not all of the operators and drivers were law-abiding, and accidents were commonplace. Ward LaFrance 202 (EDW 340) was John's favourite and during this period would be parked outside the gates of the Shaftesbury Street yard. When an incident occurred at night, as it inevitably would, the local police would call John at home to tell him where the incident was and John would call the watchman at the yard and he would walk a short distance to one of several driver's mates who lived nearby. John would meet the mate at the yard and, together, they would take the truck and drive to the incident. The police were interested only in how long it would take to get the road clear so

that traffic could start moving again – a far cry from what happens these days! Sometimes the driver would have left the scene and John would decide that the best course was to recover the errant tipper to the yard.

At one time there were 15 wrecked tipper trucks around the yard and eventually a representative of the hire purchase or leasing company that was financing the truck – or as was often the case, more than one truck – would appear and walk around the yard looking for any trucks which were 'his'. Once a truck had been located, he would be told the cost of recovery and storage and the price for delivering the damaged vehicle to his choice of location. This ensured that Wynns was never out of pocket. And if the vehicle had not been sufficiently badly damaged to warrant recovery to the yard, John would take the spare wheel back to Shaftesbury Street and, when the driver turned up looking for his wheel, he would be told what he owed Wynns for clearing his truck from the site of the accident. •

A pair of Bedford trucks intended for produce carrying. Although neither are ex-military, the left-hand vehicle, a 5-ton OW, shares the distinctive bonnet of the wartime Bedford OX and OY and was made available in small numbers to approved civilian hauliers.

Round timber extraction

Wynns became involved in the felling and extraction of round timber back in 1885 and by the early 1950s was handling more than a million cubic feet of timber a year for the local saw mills, extracting the logs from felled positions, often deep into forested areas, and subsequently carrying them to either a local mill or to the railhead.

Skilled and difficult work, it required a mix of wheeled tractors, winching vehicles and special trailers, as well as caterpillar-tracked vehicles which were used to drag felled and trimmed trees from locations which were not accessible to wheeled machinery.

In the earliest days, teams of horses were used for this work but by the 1920s they were starting to be replaced by steam traction engines. Three Sentinels, dating from 1927 and formerly owned by Williams Brothers of Pandy, were purchased for timber work in 1933, as well as a single Foden which had been new to Hire Purchase Securities two years earlier. Fowler engine number DW 2121, which had been bought new in 1920, was notably passed from the heavy-haulage fleet to timber extraction duties and survived beyond the company's centenary in 1963.

By the early 1930s, winch-equipped Scammell and Latil timber tractors were being used, the earliest record of such a machine being a rebuilt Scammell (registered UW 167, fleet number 12) which was the former property of W E Clarke & Pearce Haulage and which was rebuilt for its new role following a design laid down by Percy 'HP' Wynn. Another Scammell (DW 9735, fleet number 35) was adapted for this role in 1935.

Four Caterpillar tractors were acquired for 'tushing' – the name given to sledging round timber

New to the Forestry Commission in 1944, this Unipower Hannibal tractor was acquired by Wynns in 1947.

Far left, centre and above: Before the advent of hydraulics, extracting and loading round timber was a slow business, involving the use of chain slings and mechanical lifting equipment. Having struggled to get many tons of timber onto the telescopic pole trailer using a crane-equipped Scammell, the crew have every right to look pleased with their efforts.

A pair of Scammells work to bring a small track-laying timber tractor up a hillside. The lead vehicle, acquired in 1935, was rebuilt by Wynns especially for forestry work; the second vehicle is a Scammell six-wheeled lorry dating from 1933.

A pair of post-war Unipower Forrester timber tractors; three such vehicles were acquired by Wynns in 1950. Note the crane-equipped AEC Matador in the background.

This four-wheeled Scammell, DW 9852, was acquired in 1936 and rebuilt for forestry work.

Here, the Scammell lifts a heavy trunk onto the trailer using the mechanical crane.

This Scammell tractor is winching the loaded pole trailer up a bank.

from difficult sites. The first of these was bought new in 1938, with two more acquired second-hand in 1939, and a fourth in 1941.

A single Unipower Hannibal demonstration vehicle had been acquired in 1944 but after the end of World War 2 the timber extraction fleet was always something of a ragbag of second-hand machinery, hand-me-downs and ex-military equipment. In 1946, the company started to replace the ageing Scammells with what eventually totalled ten ex-military FWD forward-control tractors which were equipped with A-frame jibs and winches, as well as a number of Chevrolet Canadian Military Pattern (CMP) tractors. Another Caterpillar tractor was acquired in 1947,

DW 9852 coupled to a somewhat overloaded pole trailer. Note the crane folded back across the cab roof.

Unipower Forrester tractor and an ex-military FWD SU hauling timber towards the public road.

Dating from 1937, Scammell tractor ADW 616 was also converted for timber extraction by being fitted with a chain-driven winch and a small jib.

In situations where wheeled vehicles could not reach, these Caterpillar tractors could be used. The first was bought new in 1938 but others were acquired from the Forestry Commission.

purchased from the Forestry Commission, which was also the source of the company's first post-war Unipower timber tractor. Three more Caterpillars followed in 1948, another two in 1950, and two more in 1953. Three new Unipower Forrester timber tractors were also acquired in 1950. Two ex-military AEC Matadors were converted for use as timber tractors in 1958 and 1959, and an ex-military Thornycroft Nubian was also purchased for the same purpose. The last vehicle purchased especially for timber extraction work

seems to have been a Drott 'dozer acquired in August 1963.

In order to actually move the heavy timber, specialised bolster and telescopic trailers were used and these were not generally shared with the heavy-haulage activities.

Latterly, the timber fleet was based at Welshpool in mid-Wales but vehicles and equipment were also stationed at various locations across the Principality where long-term contracts were undertaken. The nature and location of the work often meant that the crews

spent days away from home and living vans were often provided on site for the duration of the work.

Timber extraction remained a vital component of the company's activities and incomes until the company's association with the timber trade ended in January 1964 when Wynns was acquired by United Transport. One of the last jobs was undertaken at Itton Court, Chepstow. At the same time, the company also withdrew from operating tipper trucks and closed the Cardiff depot. •

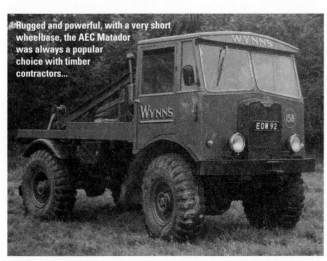

Rugged and powerful, with a very short wheelbase, the AEC Matador was always a popular choice with timber contractors...

...and Wynns was no exception. One of 12 such vehicles in service with the company, EDW 92 has been preserved.

Flashback...

Diamond T tractor number 160, registered to Wynns during May 1947, coupled to
a riveted swan-neck trailer riding on solid tyres and loaded with a 100-ton transformer.

F ollowing the end of the war in Europe in May 1945, wartime leader Winston Churchill formed a so-called 'Caretaker Government', with the Labour Party as its official opposition. Certain of his popularity and of consequent victory, Churchill called a General Election in July of that year. Sadly, he misjudged the mood of the country, and the Labour Party was swept to power with a landslide result. Churchill was relegated to opposition.

With a majority of 180, the new administration focused on what it saw as the need for greater public ownership of industry, instituting a bold and extensive programme of nationalisation. Industries such as coal-mining, railways, steel-making, canals, gas, electricity, the Bank of England… and road haulage – all of which were described by the Labour administration as 'decaying and unprofitable' – were to be nationalised.

The Road Haulage Association (RHA), which represented the owners of the industry, was bitterly opposed to nationalisation, as were the Conservative and Liberal Parties, although the latter did support the nationalisation of the railways. The RHA began to distribute propaganda and put up posters across the country. A 25-minute film extolling the virtues of private ownership was shown more than 3,000 times in halls all over the country, with viewers being asked to sign a petition against the proposed nationalisation of the industry.

In November 1946, the 'Transport Bill' was put before Parliament, seeking to transfer the railways, canals and most long-distance road haulage into state ownership. The resulting Act established the British Transport Commission (BTC), giving it powers to acquire transport undertakings as it felt necessary and the BTC came into operation on 1 January 1948, with Lord Hurcomb as its first Chairman, and Miles Beevor as Chief Secretary. Shares in the railway companies were exchanged for British Transport Stock, with a guaranteed 3 per cent return chargeable to the BTC. Compensation for former railway shareholders was based on the valuation of the railway companies in 1946, a time when the railways were in a dilapidated state because of war damage and minimal maintenance. Its main holdings were the networks and assets of the 'Big Four' regional railway companies – the Great Western Railway (GWR), the London and North Eastern Railway (LNER), the London, Midland and Scottish Railway (LMS), and the Southern Railway (SR). It also took over 55 other railway undertakings and 19 canal operating companies. The BTC went on to become one of the largest industrial organisations in the world, at one time employing nearly 688,000 people, with its influence spreading into almost every aspect of transportation in Britain.

Road haulage also came under the remit of the BTC as did the work of the London

A four-wheel Scammell draw-bar unit, acquired in September 1954, helps a Diamond T with a Marshall boiler unit in a confined space. In this situation, the rear tractor provides help with steering as well as motive power.

Despite being Newport-registered and driven by Wynns' crews, these Thornycroft Mighty Antar ballast tractors were destined for Australia where they were used to haul electrical equipment for the Snowy Mountains Hydro-Electric Scheme. The Wynns' men were contracted to train the Australian crews.

The challenges of Nationalisation

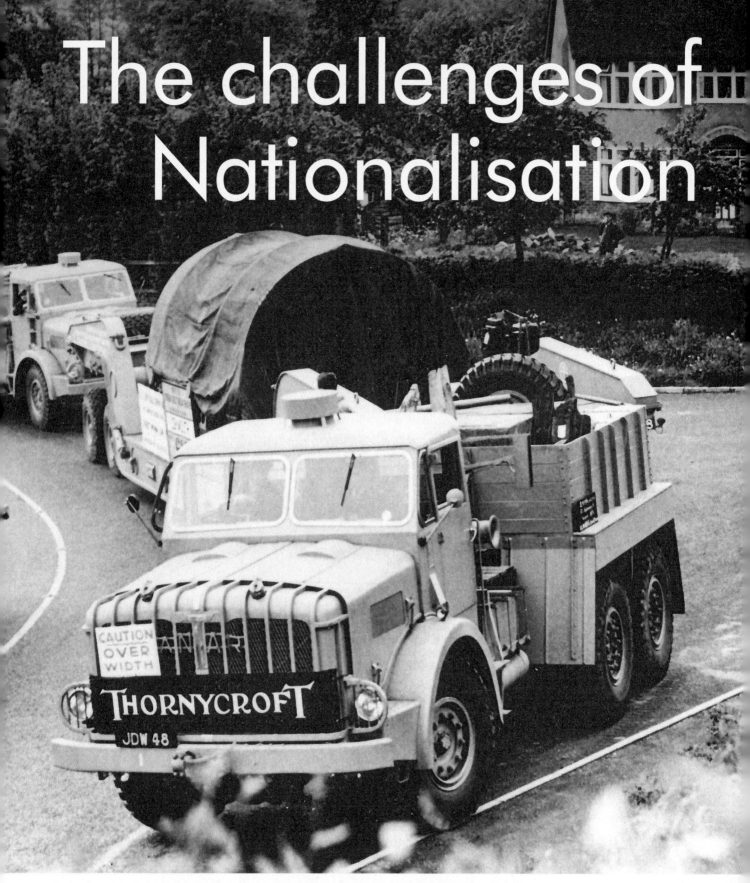

Passenger Transport Board (LPTB), which was already publicly owned. But it seems that the RHA's lobbying had not entirely been in vain because on 13 March 1947 the Minister for Transport, Alfred Barnes, had told the Standing Committee that he intended to remove the clauses from the Bill which limited the operation of 'C' licensed vehicles.

At the time there were three types of licence issued to hauliers: the 'A' licence was for public carriers; the 'B' licence for traders carrying the goods of others as well as their own; and the 'C' licence was used by traders transporting their own goods up to a radius of 40 miles from their operating base. Although the decision undermined his original objective that all long-distance road haulage would be carried by the proposed state-owned road-haulage company, this is how the Bill was passed into law as the 'Transport Act 1947'. The local road distribution networks of the pre-nationalisation rail companies, as well as the removals company Pickfords, which had previously been owned jointly by the railways, were all nationalised, as were a further 246 smaller independent companies who were predominantly engaged in ordinary long-distance work. For the purposes of the Act, this was considered to include operators who covered distances of 40 miles or upwards.

Altogether, some 246 haulage firms were nationalised, including the removals company Pickfords which had merged with Carter Patterson in 1946 to form Joint Parcels Service, and which, by virtue of being owned by the railway companies, had already been nationalised in 1947. The 'light' and 'medium' operators were later re-organised as British Road Services (BRS), but the name Pickfords began to appear on all of the vehicles of the former 'heavy' operators, including Box, E W Rudd, Gavin Wilkie, Siddle Cook, and others.

However, any transport business which could show that more than half of its income came from 'exempted traffic' was permitted to remain in private hands; such traffic included meat, furniture, bulk liquids and round timber... and, fortunately for Wynns, heavy haulage.

Despite losing their nightly London-South Wales trunk routes, by virtue of having bought a fleet of tankers which had formerly been operated by Powell Duffryn, and then subcontracting them to the newly-created National Coal Board (NCB), Wynns was able to increase their exempted traffic beyond the relevant figure and thus was able to escape the net. The company was not paid any compensation for the loss of the trunk routes for almost three years and, whilst this state of affairs may have been fine for Wynns who had other work, it can't have been good for other, smaller, operators. Many of their competitors were less fortunate and were absorbed into the Pickfords' undertaking.

The Labour Government continued apace with its nationalisation plan for the selected industries and, by 1951, some 20 per cent of the national economy was controlled by the state, employing a workforce of over two million. Whether or not these moves were approved by the majority of the electorate is a moot point but the Labour Government was ousted in that same year in favour of a new Conservative administration led by Winston Churchill. The Conservatives called a halt to the programme of nationalisation and the road haulage industry was eventually de-nationalised and de-regulated, although the still heavily-regulated railways and buses were left under the control of the BTC.

In practice, nationalisation had destroyed the industry and, for many years, little on the ground changed. Wynns, which had always remained in private hands, together with the nationalised Pickfords company, had the heavy-haulage field all to themselves until the late 1950s when

Rated at 150-200 tons, and loaded with an enormous 146-ton dragline excavator, trailer 444 requires five tractors to haul it up the incline, including a Ward LaFrance wrecker, a Foden and a Pacific pulling, together with a Scammell draw-bar tractor and a Pacific at the rear.

they were joined by Sunters of Northallerton.

Competition between Wynns and Pickfords was fierce and, as previously recounted, Percy Wynn was delighted to be able to snaffle the contract for delivering the 105-ton Indian railway locomotive to the Festival of Britain. In truth Wynns was not in a position to undertake the job since the company lacked suitable equipment. In conjunction with Fairfields at Chepstow, Percy had to oversee the design and construction of a pair of carrying beams in just two months. However, the high profile and prestigious nature of this contract more than anything helped to put Wynns firmly on the map as an extremely capable haulier, able to deal with the heaviest and most difficult loads.

Whilst Wynns undoubtedly quickly acquired considerable expertise in handling unusual loads, the company

also always seemed to be able to come up with the right piece of equipment for the job. Credit for this should be given to Percy Wynn who was in charge of vehicle procurement and engineering at the time. It was Percy who pioneered the use of steered trailers and Percy who first specified pneumatic tyres for extreme loads, having seen a model produced by the trailer manufacturers Cranes of Dereham.

At the beginning of the 1950s it was standard practice for any outfit hauling an abnormal load to deploy a 'pusher' truck at the rear, not only to help with the weight, but also using the second tractor to steer the rear of the trailer which would otherwise tend to cut across corners. The downside of this was that it made the outfit longer than was often necessary and careful co-ordination was always required by the drivers of the two tractors. In an attempt to get around this, trailer-makers Cranes

Acquired in 1941 under special Ministry of Transport licence, CDW 910 was an ERF tractor unit for use with semi-trailers.

Scammell provided the bulk of the medium haulage fleet during the early post-war years. Here, a typical tractor unit, new to British Road Services in July 1952, is seen coupled to a flat-bed trailer loaded with steel tubes.

of Dereham had been working on the development of a heavy trailer which would incorporate hydraulic steering and hydraulic suspension, an additional bonus of which was that the suspension could also be used to raise and lower the trailer frame, replacing the tedious practice of using separate jacks. It was also planned that the trailer would run on pneumatic tyres rather than the 'solids' which had been normal practice up to that time.

The tyres were developed in conjunction with Dunlop, who had produced a 16.00-20 24-ply tyre rated for a load of ten tons at 5mph and 7.5 tons at 12mph... with 16 of these tyres, a trailer could carry 120 tons.

Cranes showed a scale model of such a trailer to Percy Wynn – and to Pickfords – at the 1951 Commercial Motor Show. He immediately saw the potential for this development, and insisted that Cranes build such a trailer

for Wynns. Whilst happily accepting the order, neither Cranes nor Dunlop was prepared to offer any guarantee that the trailer would be satisfactory at full scale and the operation was, effectively, undertaken entirely at Wynns' expense since the company would have had no comeback if the trailer proved to be unsatisfactory. However, Percy had stolen a march on the nationalised Pickfords which, with its necessarily more bureaucratic approach, needed more time to evaluate the trailer and to raise the necessary paperwork. It was the procurement of this trailer which effectively put Wynns and Pickfords head-to-head.

Having placed his order, Percy wanted to see the job through and often made the long trip to Cranes workshops in Norfolk where he could be found checking on the progress of the trailer (which was eventually allocated fleet number 333) during

construction. John felt that he was equally involved since, despite being just 19 at the time, he was Percy's chauffeur and he always drove the older man to Dereham. The journey was close to 250 miles and, in those distant days before the motorways were built, must have taken a full seven or eight hours. At first John drove Percy's Ford V8 Pilot, but this was eventually replaced by a Ford Zephyr Mk 1, and finally by a succession of Jaguars. In fact Percy's first Jaguar, a Mk VII, was purchased in Nottingham when he was attending one of the sales of ex-military vehicles at Ruddington and when this Mk VII was replaced by a second example, in the same colour, Percy arranged for the same numberplate, RTV 990, to be retained. This was not a common practice in those days and when John asked him why he had done it, Percy replied that he didn't want customers thinking that the company was earning too much. The plate was even retained following the arrival of a third Mk VII in two-tone blue but, by this time, John thought that perhaps most customers might have got the idea!

When they saw what the trailer could do, Pickfords eventually followed suit, ordering a similar 16-wheel 120-ton unit which effectively forced Wynns to go one better. In 1952, Percy persuaded Cranes and Dunlop to construct a 24-wheel 150-200 ton version of this trailer. This particular trailer, fleet number 444, utilised the two eight-wheel bogies of trailer 333 but with the addition of an extra line of four wheels on each bogie giving wheel centres of 75 inches and 61 inches. Cranes then built new swan necks and a pair of 30-foot long 36-inch deep girders. Naturally, 'HP' made use of the (now surplus) frame of trailer 333 by having Cranes build a new pair of non-hydraulic eight-wheel bogies to produce a very versatile 150-ton trailer (fleet number 500).

Trailer 444 entered service on 30 May 1954 and was used to successfully move six 150-ton transformers from the British Thompson Houston (BTH) works at Rugby to locations around the country where the Central Electricity Generating Board (CEGB) was constructing power stations. And, when the CEGB indicated that there was a need for still-heavier loads to be moved, Wynns wasted no time and came up with a 28-wheel 200-ton trailer, which used a pair of additional castor wheels under the swan necks to help carry the load... an idea which Percy had come up with.

For many years the two companies were constantly battling for supremacy. The 200-ton figure remained the

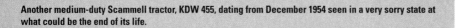

Another medium-duty Scammell tractor, KDW 455, dating from December 1954 seen in a very sorry state at what could be the end of its life.

Even with the benefit of hydraulic steering on the trailer bogies, it often needed all of the available road space to negotiate a corner. This is one of the Cranes trailers, similar to Wynns' 333, supplied for the Snowy Mountains Scheme. Having seen the route and the terrain involved the Australian crews asked if the Wynns' men would bring the outfit down and they would ride with them, acting merely as observers.

practical upper limit until the mid-sixties when Wynns purchased a 300-ton trailer (fleet number 789) from Cranes running on two eight-row bogies, with two separate two-row bogies able to be fitted when required to provide the maximum 300-ton capacity. There was no question now as to the supremacy and reliability of pneumatic tyres and the trailer wheels were shod with 8.25-15 tyres.

During the 1950s Wynns was scarcely short of heavy-haulage work, with transformers, excavators, generators, railway locomotives and sundry chemical plant being produced all over the country which needed delivery. And, in an ironic twist of fate, three and sometimes four DiamondTs and tank-transporter trailers were working continuously for at least two years moving tanks for the Ministry of Supply – some were new, others destined to be broken for scrap and the operation finally came to an end when the supply of scrap tanks dried up. New Wynns' depots were opened at Manchester and Chasetown to augment the existing Newport, Cardiff, and London locations, and there was also a timber-extraction depot at Welshpool.

In 1953, the company's growing expertise in heavy haulage was recognised when Wynns was asked by representatives of the Snowy

Mountains Hydro-Electric Scheme to recommend a trailer and tractors for export to Australia where they were to be used for hauling heavy electrical equipment. Wynns recommended a Cranes 16-wheel trailer, similar to fleet number 333, and the Australians placed an order with Cranes for what was the third trailer of this type. As regards the tractor, Wynns suggested that the Scammell Constructor would be suitable but, presumably price became a consideration and, in the end, the Australians opted for a pair of Thornycroft Mighty Antars. This was

not the end of Wynns' involvement and the company was later asked to test and license the Mighty Antars in conjunction with this trailer and to train the Australian crews.

The Mighty Antar had been developed in 1949 for hauling sections of steel oil pipe across the Iraqi desert from Homs to Kirkuk, but the design had quickly been adopted by the British Army as an 'off the shelf' tank transporter to replace and supplement the ageing DiamondTs. The first British Army Antars were steel-bodied ballast tractors, but in 1952 Thornycroft started

A selection of Wynns' tippers photographed in 1961; in January 1964 the company withdrew from operating tipper trucks and closed the Cardiff depot.

Lifting an 8-ton lifeboat aboard the *FS Campanda* at Southampton as part of the Festival of Britain exhibition in 1951.

Scammell Mountaineer draw-bar tractor, dating from 1957, coupled to a low-loader trailer carrying a Metrovick railway locomotive destined for the South African Railways.

work on developing the Mk 2 military Antar which was eventually produced in both fifth-wheel and ballast tractor form. Perhaps it was the use of the Antar as a tank transporter that impressed the Australians but, whatever the reason, a contract was placed for a pair of wooden-bodied ballast tractors – chassis numbers 54780 and 54781 – similar to the military Mk 2 specification. Like the military versions, these two tractors were powered by the huge Rover V8 Meteorite engine – in compression-ignition configuration rather than the fuel-injected petrol version favoured by the British Army. Transmission was the standard Thornycroft 4F1Rx3 arrangement that put 12 speeds at the disposal of a nimble driver who had learned the art of split changing. A 50,000 lb Darlington winch was fitted behind the cab; air-brake connections were provided at front and rear for double-heading and, unusually, the connections were conveniently placed to allow the brakes to be operated whilst the tractors were pushing the massive trailer sideways.

It was arranged that the Australian crews would come over to the UK, as the contractor wanted, quite naturally, to have the outfit road-tested before being exported. Wynns had secured an order to move six 120-ton inner stators from GEC at Whitton, Birmingham to the Uskmouth A Power Station in Newport and it seemed that this would provide an ideal training exercise for the Australians. Wynns collected the trailer from Cranes and delivered it to GEC using one of their own tractors, whilst the Antars were collected from the Thornycroft works at Basingstoke and were also driven by Wynns' crews to Birmingham. To operate legally in the UK, both tractors had to be licensed and the two plates were JDW 48 and JDW 49.

The Australian crew was driven up to Birmingham, over the road that they would have to travel but, on seeing the route and the terrain involved – no motorways, if you remember, in those days – the men asked if one of the Wynns' crews would bring the outfit down and they would ride with them, acting merely as observers. Bill Pitton drove the lead tractor and Wilf Wedlake drove the pusher – Kipper Kent was the steersman. The journey was accomplished without incident, but negotiating the corner at Monmouth was, as always, a very tricky manoeuvre, with the front tractor uncoupled to gain maximum headroom. Neither of the Wynns' drivers was greatly impressed with the Antars but, in all fairness, they were the first in production and, of course, the forward-control Cummins-powered Pacifics which Wynns would have used for a job like this were without equal at the time.

By the time the move was over, the trucks were well proven, but the crews returned to 'Oz' with no actual driving experience at all!

In passing, it is worth noting that the Snowy Mountains Hydro-Electric Scheme was one of the most complex water and electricity projects in the world, and entailed capturing the waters of the Snowy River and its tributary, the Eucumbene, at high elevations, and completely reversing the flow of the Snowy River westwards into the interior rather than eastwards into the Pacific. The waters of these two rivers were then joined with the Murray and Murrumbidgee rivers through two tunnel systems driven through the bedrock of the Snowy Mountains. To drive the turbines, the water fell 2,500 feet through large hydro-electric power stations which would generate peak-load electrical power for New South Wales and Victoria. The scheme took 25 years to complete and was not fully operational until 1974.

No doubt Thornycroft had hoped that exposing Wynns to the Mighty Antar would lead to some examples of this very capable tractor being purchased to replace Wynns' ageing Diamond Ts. Sadly for the Basingstoke-based company, Wynns remained loyal to Scammell and although no examples of Thornycroft's Mighty Antar joined the Wynns' fleet on a permanent basis, this was certainly a period of acquisition. Ex-military vehicles continued to join the growing Wynns' fleet during the 1950s and other vehicles acquired during this period included more than a dozen Scammell draw-bar tractors, some new, some secondhand, including a pair of Mountaineers... as well as 14 Bedford KHTC 8-ton tippers.

From the end of 1959, the company was also appointed as the main South Wales dealer for Guy Motors. Not only did this give them access to some of Guy's prototypes but it also made it easier to acquire production trucks.

It was also during this period that Wynns had gained a contract from the Newport-based company Stewart & Lloyds who were producing pipeline sections for the incoming North Sea gas grid being installed by Pipeline Contractors Limited (PLC). Wynns had already been moving the 40-foot long pipe sections using artic trailers which had been specially lengthened from 27 feet to 40 feet by Wynns' workshop welder, Bryn Lavender but, as the volume of work increased, 36 Guy Invincible and Big J tractors were

Wynns was appointed as the main dealer for Guy Motors in South Wales and had a chance to try most of the company's products. A fleet of these unusual Invincible bonneted tractors was acquired for medium-duty haulage from 1960.

purchased, together with some new Northern trailers especially for this contract.

By the end of the decade, Wynns was close to celebrating its centenary and, as the company's reputation for shifting impossible loads spread, had already started working overseas. However, the five Wynn brothers were approaching retirement age and the death of Sam Wynn in July 1962 and the subsequent bill for death duties cast something of a pall over the company. John and his cousin Noel were appointed as directors but there was some question regarding the ability of the two men to run what had become a sizeable business and one which had previously been run by what was effectively a team of five.

After more than a decade in Government hands, road haulage was about to be privatised under Harold

Macmillan's 'Transport Act 1962'. But the Conservatives were tired, having been in power for almost all of the 1950s, and there was a lingering possibility that any new Labour Government would resume the programme of nationalisation that had been abandoned in 1951. If the growth which Wynns had enjoyed during the 1950s was to be continued into the new decade, the company needed additional capital. One possibility was a flotation on the London Stock Exchange but this would have meant that the family would have to relinquish control and if this were to happen, the directors believed that it would be better to sell the business outright. Overtures were made by both Pickfords and United Transport, and Pickfords (by now in the hands of the Transport Holding Company rather than the British Transport

Although never particularly successful, the Guy Invincible was available as both a truck and tractor, with two, three or four axles. Here, an Invincible tractor unit is couple to low-loading trailer 433 which carries the body of a large excavator.

Scammell Highwayman tractor unit dating from 1965 coming off the Red Funnel ferry *Carisbrooke Castle* with a transformer load collected from Shanklin.

Commission) would certainly have jumped at the chance of taking on Wynns' operations.

Although Pickfords had made the better offer, the family was not keen for the business to fall into the hands of their erstwhile competitor and, anyway, United Transport had guaranteed that the name Wynns would not be lost. Accordingly, in 1962, the Wynns' Board of directors started serious discussions with United Transport who were seeking expansion in the British road haulage sector.

However, Wynns was approaching its centenary and the board wanted to celebrate this important milestone as a family-owned firm and organised an impressive parade of vehicles through the streets of Newport.

The parade was originally the idea of the then-Deputy Chief Constable Wally Newton who, nevertheless, was keen that traffic was not disrupted. Enthusiastic crowds watched as a convoy of Wynns' machinery, including a horse and cart and a Fowler steam traction engine dating from 1920, brought normal traffic on the streets of the town to a standstill. Standing in Westgate Square, 'HP' took the salute as the procession of red-painted trucks and trailers rolled by and the company showed what it could do to the people of the town that had been its home for 100 years.

It was not until a few months later, in February 1964, that the sale of Wynns to Bulwark United Transport of Chepstow was announced. The

chairmanship passed to David Lloyd-Jones, with Robert ('RT') Wynn as his deputy. Percy and Gordon Wynn were joint General Managers, and Noel and John Wynn were also appointed to the Board, with the 34-year old John beginning to take on the role of vehicle procurement from 'HP'... his Uncle Percy. George Wynn elected for retirement but remained on the Board.

At the same time, the Welshpool depot was sold separately, along with the timber-extraction business, and Wynns also withdrew from tipper work, closing the Cardiff depot. Despite these changes and upheavals, Wynns continued to prosper and the early 1960s saw an expansion of the company's activities, both at home and, increasingly, overseas. •

A pair of large cylindrical rolls or stator units being loaded and secured. The trucks on show include three Diamond Ts and a Scammell.

Heavy-haulage Contractors

For the two decades following the end of World War 2, the Pacific and Diamond T tractors had provided the mainstay of Wynns' heavy-haulage fleet. The inevitable ravages of time were kept at bay by a programme of constant modification and it would be fair to say that by the end of their lives these vehicles would have been unrecognisable to their makers.

However, by the mid-1960s, it was obvious that the old warriors were nearing the end of their useful lives and that newer and more capable machinery was required. The new owners of the company, United Transport, sanctioned the purchase of a fleet of new heavy tractors.

By this time, Scammell and Thornycroft were the only British manufacturers capable of producing such machines... although perhaps it would be more true to say that Scammell remained the only company actually building heavy tractors.

Thornycroft had built their last Mighty Antar in 1963 and, although there was talk of an Antar Mk 4, nothing was ever to come of this. And, anyway, both companies were now part of the Leyland Group. Scammell had been absorbed in 1955, and Thornycroft, via its association with ACV, in 1962. The two companies remained on separate sites until 1969, with Scammell at Watford and Thornycroft some 50 miles away at Basingstoke, but Thornycroft's design team was effectively absorbed into the Scammell operation.

Wynns had operated plenty of Scammells in the 1930s, and had also purchased a handful of medium-sized Scammell tractors after the war for both draw-bar and fifth-wheel operation. Unlike Pickfords and Sunters, Wynns had never purchased examples of the Scammell Constructor which had

appeared in 1952... although Pickfords had used the Constructor to replace their ageing Diamond Ts. And, despite trialling such a machine, Wynns had not acquired the more-powerful Super Constructor which had joined the range in 1958, still preferring their home-brewed Pacific and Diamond T tractors. All of the Wynns' Pacific drivers had been given a chance to drive the Super Constructor, which had been a temporary member of the Wynns' fleet for three months, and even 'HP' had driven it for a half-day coupled to trailer 666. All agreed that it was no match for the mighty Pacifics.

However, the announcement of

Scammell's magnificent Contractor in 1964 coincided with the need to replace the ageing American machines and, this time, Wynns certainly sat up and took notice.

The Contractor was intended to replace the Constructor but it was a huge step forward. As well as being Scammell's most-

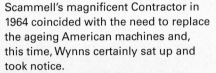

powerful tractor to date, it went on to become the most successful heavy tractor produced by the company in its history. Designed for towing either draw-bar or semi-trailers, the 'baby' of the range was rated at 100 tons, with 125/150-ton and 240-ton versions also available, the latter identifiable by its larger rear hubs and heavier-duty tyres. During its near 20-year production life the Contractor was offered with Rolls-Royce and Cummins engines rated from 300 to 450bhp and with manual, semi-automatic or automatic transmissions; one intrepid operator even specified

a Detroit Diesel engine. Wynns chose to stick with the tried and tested Cummins.

The first Wynns' Contractor (fleet number 188, registration FDW 769E) was one of four 100-ton tractors purchased over a two-year period. It cost the company somewhere around £80,000 – which is worth a staggering £1.1 million at today's prices – and was delivered in 1966. Resplendent in its Wynns' livery, the vehicle appeared on the Scammell stand at the 1966 Commercial Motor Show at London's Earls Court where it attracted huge attention. And what a fine piece of work the Contractor was… coupled together, two or three of these powerful and capable machines could easily haul more than 300 tons or more. Indeed, in his book *Scammell the Load Movers from Watford*, Nick Georgano reports that Highland Fabricators of Ross-shire regularly

The Scammell Contractor was a technological leap forward and was the first commercial tractor that Wynns believed could replace their much-modified Pacifics. Here *Crusader*, a 240-ton Mk 1 tractor from 1969, handles one of three enormous pressure vessels for the Shell refinery at Stanlow.

Contractor *Resolute*, acquired in 1974, coupled to a 10-line flat-topped trailer travelling at what passes for motorway speed in heavy-haulage terms.

One of the smaller, 100-ton Contractors handles a load on a lengthy swan-necked trailer destined for Allis Chalmers in Pennsylvania.

A pair of 240-ton Contractors handle a 14-axle trailer carrying a 450-ton vessel, the largest of 21 such units carried for Blaesbjerg UK destined for the Mobil refinery at Coryton, Essex.

Rex Farrell of the CEGB developed a method of carrying heavy transformers on a special 48-wheeled air-lift – or 'hover' – trailer which reduced axle loadings, and thus avoided rebuilding bridges. Trailers 789, 987 and 999 were adapted to work with the blower equipment.

used a pair of Contractors to move loads of up to 1,600 tons over short distances... although admittedly, off the public highway!

Early Contractors were powered by a 12.17-litre Rolls-Royce Eagle diesel engine, with the option of Cummins units (ultimately the range included the NH220, NH250, NT335, NT380 and the NT400), and most were constructed in 6x4 configuration with the massive rear bogie driven through either a Fuller 15-speed gearbox, or an eight-speed Self Changing Gears RV30 semi-automatic unit in combination with an optional two-speed epicyclic splitter which gave the driver 15 very-closely-spaced ratios to play with. The axles were 40-ton Kirkstall Forge units with epicyclic reduction gearing in the hubs.

As regards suspension, Scammell had long since abandoned their innovative walking-beam suspension and the Contractor featured massive inverted semi-elliptical multi-leaf springs.

Wynns' early 100-ton vehicles, and most of the 150-ton vehicles, were fitted with a two-door Motor Panels cab, seating three across, but later vehicles were fitted with four-door crew cabs capable of accommodating the whole crew of up to eight men. The company favoured left-hand drive... perhaps in deference to the kerb-crawling lives which these heavy tractors often led, or perhaps it was a nod to the similarly-controlled Diamond Ts and Pacifics to which the Wynns' drivers had become accustomed... and let's face it, Wynns' drivers were unlikely to be doing a lot of overtaking. All of Wynn's Contractors were delivered with ballast bodies, initially carrying a full-width body which proved to be something of a problem.

One Saturday morning, John Wynn had the chance of driving Tommy Cromwell's tractor (Wynns' fleet number 182, NDW 836G) on London's North Circular road. The tractor was coupled to trailer 789 loaded with a 180-ton transformer and John recalls that it was pouring with rain. He complained immediately that the width of the ballast box restricted vision to the rear and, with direct experience of the problems that this could cause, at the next Board meeting John was able to persuade his fellow directors that future deliveries should be fitted with narrower bodies. These smaller bodies forced Wynns to abandon their customary loose steel-shot ballast in favour of Scammell's more conventional cast weights which, of course, increased the price of the trucks.

Between 1966 and 1981, Wynns took delivery of 25 Mk 1 Contractors. Although all were initially equipped with ballast boxes, a number were

Challenger, one of the 240-ton Contractors, negotiates a roundabout the wrong way with a 177-ton transformer on its way to Manchester Docks. A 100-ton Contractor brings up the rear.

subsequently retro-fitted with a fifth-wheel in Wynns' workshops for use with a semi-trailer *(see page 67)* and may even have also been converted back again. As had become the custom, and in the style of railway locomotives, most of the tractors were named and, as had been the case with the Pacifics, it was John himself who decided on a series of suitably heroic names.

The company's great rivals over at Pickfords also chose to buy the Contractor, taking delivery of their first example in 1967, as did almost any company with aspirations in the heavy-haulage business... including Sunters, Wrekin Roadways, Siddle Cook, and the South Africa-based Thorntons who, like Wynns, were ultimately taken into the United Group of Companies.

The Contractor was also offered as a 6x4 and 6x6 tank transporter, with examples certainly supplied to Jordan and perhaps Iran. The British Army did not operate any Contractors as tank transporters, although the Royal Electrical and Mechanical Engineers (REME) did acquire one, which has now passed into preservation.

A total of 1,257 Contractors were built between 1966 and 1983, with 73 of these sold in Britain... the bulk of domestic sales going to Wynns and Pickfords. Of this total figure, just six were of the Mk 2 version, which was eventually superseded, almost by default, by the Scammell S24. Only six Mk 2s are said to have been constructed; four going to Wynns and two to Pickfords.

In passing, and in one of those ironic twists of fate that make history such a fascinating subject, it is worth pointing out that, in effect, there eventually *was* an Antar Mk 4 because, under the able direction of Don Pearson, with assistance from John Fadell and Mike Ballard, the combined efforts of Scammell and Thornycroft designers produced what was effectively a son of Contractor and Antar... the British Army's Scammell Commander. Sadly, by 1987 Scammell had succumbed to the world-wide recession and fell into the hands of Unipower, and later Alvis, with a very restricted product offering.

Suspended on a pair of six-line bogies, 240-ton *Resolute* carries a large transformer on a pair of deep swan-necks.

Technical specification
Scammell Contractor Mks1-3

Identification

Manufacturer:
Scammell Lorries Limited;
Watford, Hertfordshire.

Manufacturer's designation:
Contractor Mks 1-3.

Production: 1966-83.

Number produced:
1,257 approximately.

Number in service with Wynns: 28.

Specification

Engine (as specified by Wynns):
Cummins NH220, NH250, NT335,
NT385 or NT400; six cylinders in-line;
diesel, NT335, NT385 and NT400,
turbocharged; water-cooled; 12,170cc
(NH220), 14,010cc (NH250, NT335,
NT385, and NT400); overhead valves;
power output, 212bhp at 1,300rpm,
rising to 375bhp at 2,100rpm,
according to engine. Other engines
also available.

Transmission: Leyland six- or seven-
speed manual, the latter with two-
speed splitter box; Fuller 15-speed
manual; or Self Changing Gears
RV30 eight-speed semi-automatic
unit, with an optional two-speed
epicyclic splitter.

Drive line: 6x4.

Suspension: live axles on multi-leaf
semi-elliptical springs.

Brakes: air pressure.

Electrical system: 24V.

Dimensions

Length, 306in; **width,** 98in;
height, 116in.

Wheelbase: 218in.

Bogie centres: 63in.

Weight: unladen (minimum),
27,647 lb; authorised gross train
weight, 100,000-160,000 lb.

Performance: maximum speed,
50mph.

Challenger, seen here negotiating a 370-ton, 144-foot long platform reactor after delivery to Shellhaven.

Twenty-axle flat-topped trailer carrying a reactor column manufactured by Japan Steel Works for Shell. The load is being pulled by 240-ton Contractor *Challenger* and pushed by a second Contractor.

A pair of six-line bogies being used to receive a 140-ton, 16-foot diameter vessel destined for the Amoco refinery at Milford haven in 1972. The trailers are being nosed into the correct position by 240-ton Contractor *Challenger*.

The three pressure vessels intended for the Shell refinery at Stanlow were the largest loads to be carried on British roads at that time, the largest weighing 212 tons. Constructed in the Netherlands, the vessels were off-loaded from the Gloria Sidrum at Birkenhead and moved 17 miles in convoy. Here, the 240-ton Conqueror is pulling, with a second, 100-ton, Contractor at the rear.

However, the inclusion of the Scammell Contractor in the Wynns' fleet was a turning point for both companies, leading to a collaboration which saw Wynns contribute to the development of the more-powerful Mk 2 Contractor and, at this point, it might be worth describing the first Wynns' tractor named *Dreadnought*... Pacific number 192 (GDW 277). This tractor was rebuilt on a Scammell Contractor chassis and subsequently re-registered as NDW 345G and it was this vehicle which led Wynns' engineer Stan Anderson to order a Contractor in the mid-1970s to be delivered without engine and transmission. Having gained experience with the hybrid Pacific/Scammell, Stan intended to produce a more-powerful customised truck that he believed would better suit the company's needs. In the end the Contractor Mk 2, as it became known, was developed jointly by Wynns and Scammell and, despite being rated at a conservative 250 tons, with its 450bhp Cummins engine and Allison automatic gearbox, was more than capable of hauling up to 450 tons. There had previously been some resistance among the crews to the use of automatic transmission but, by fitting such a system to Pacific tractor 195, 'HP' had proved that there were no potential problems.

Interestingly, the Mk 2 Contractor lacked the normal Jacobs' engine brake (the so-called 'Jake brake') but used a pedal-operated retarder instead. This demanded an unusual driving

Two Contractors were required, with *Talisman* in the lead, to move this 105ft-long boiler drum weighing 251 tons.

technique that required the driver to rev the engine on downhill stretches to engage the brake... which must have gone against every instinct! The first of the Mk 2s (Wynns' fleet number 602, RWO 73R) had been given to Roger Barnfield, in conjunction with trailer 987, the longest trailer in the fleet. Stan Anderson had been taking a lot of flak from 'HP' because Roger, who had no faith in the way that the retarder operated, kept complaining about the braking capabilities of the new truck. Stan approached John and asked him if

he would prove that the new retarder worked properly so, one Sunday morning John left his home with his wife Maureen, and drove to Stafford where Roger had loaded a 256-ton stator, destined for the USA, onto the trailer. John took over the driving on the A34 north of Stafford. With two Mk 1 Contractors pushing, the load crested the incline and John gave the bell signal to the rear tractors to stop pushing as the load started on the first downgrade. Roger was sitting in the mate's seat and was watching John closely as he did exactly what Stan Anderson had briefed him to do. John reports a heart-stopping couple of minutes before he felt the retarder start to do its job... but there were to be no more complaints.

Until the general downturn of the late 1970s, Wynns' Contractors were never short of work... stators, transformers, railway locomotives, excavators, chemical plant, bridge sections, concrete beams, and all manner of industrial plant. If a heavy or unusual load needed moving... anywhere in the world... then Wynns were in a position to do it.

One particularly interesting load was a 220-ton boiler drum destined for Littlebrook 'D' Power Station. The boiler was loaded onto new seven- and ten-line Nicolas trailers at the works of John Thompson (Wolverhampton) Limited by Ern Adams and his gang using new powered-beam jacks and a 240-ton Contractor was coupled to each end of the trailer giving a total length of 100 feet. On Sunday 6 August 1976, John and his wife Maureen drove to Wolverhampton and John took the wheel of the lead tractor, *Talisman* (registration HHB 361N, Wynns' fleet number 196), for some four or five hours, leaving the outfit north of Stafford. Three such loads were carried like this.

Wynns was also the first company to use the air-cushion equipment on the Felin Puleston railway bridge on the A483 at Wrexham while delivering a 155-ton AEI transformer to the Legacy

Grid site in February 1967. Developed in conjunction with CEGB engineer Rex Farrell, the air-cushion equipment was designed to reduce axle loadings on weak bridges, and was subsequently pressed into action by Wynns on more than 1,000 occasions, notably on shifting a series of 258-ton GEC-built stators destined for Didcot, Hinkley Point 'B', Hartlepool and Heysham Power Stations.

A dozen 233-ton transformers were built by GEC Power Engineering Limited at Stafford and delivered to Pembroke and Didcot Power Stations using a new end-suspension system. The special swan necks were designed and manufactured by GEC and the transformer was placed in a drop-frame carrier suspended on six-axle bogies at either end, taken from trailer 789, that eliminated the need for the main carrying beams. With a pair of Contractors providing the motive power, the entire journey from Didcot to Pomona Dock at Manchester for onward transport by Ro-Ro to Pembroke was conducted at a maximum speed of 10mph.

Another challenging load was a T-shaped pressure vessel with a maximum width of 35ft combined with a length of 66ft... the 108-ton load was easily handled by a single Contractor but the four-mile move on the Ministry of Defence's Pendine Proof & Experimental Establishment site involved the removal of power lines and sundry road works to accommodate the width.

The largest of three vessels destined for the Shell refinery at Stanlow weighed 212 tons and had a maximum diameter of 25ft.

It is also worth describing the largest load which Wynns carried on British roads. Three enormous pressure vessels, which had been built in the Netherlands, were moved 17 miles

Driver Roger Banfield runs alongside *Talisman*. The load is a 251-ton boiler drum destined for Littlebrook D Power Station.

from Cammell Laird at Birkenhead to the Shell refinery at Stanlow in a most impressive convoy. No one at Wynns had made the trip to the Netherlands to look at these pressure vessels and John was horrified when they arrived at Birkenhead on the *Gloria Sidrum*. The policeman in charge of supervising the move, Chief Inspector Des Southwell, reacted stoically when he was told by John Wynn, at three minutes to 6.00am on the morning of 5 December, that he would not move the load out of Cammell Laird's yard that day despite the fact that three footbridges had been dismantled on the route and countless 'keep left' signs and other street furniture had been removed in preparation for the 17-mile journey. "OK", he said, giving John a long hard look before he stood down the 30 motorcycle policemen who were ready to accompany the load, "you know best". It was to be another two weeks before the extra bogies that were required were hired from Stoof Transport in the Netherlands, but the move then went off without a hitch. One of the vessels weighed 212 tons and measured 112ft in length and 25ft in diameter, and the move was effected using double-width six-axle bogies under each end of the vessel, with Contractors both pushing and pulling.

It was during the planning operations for this project some 18 months earlier that John Wynn had met Ron Swenson of the American Fluor Corporation, who was in charge of the operation, and who was effectively Wynns' client. The two men struck up a lasting friendship that endures to this day and, with their respective wives, there have been many visits both to John's home in South Wales and Ron's home in California. Similarly, even though he later tried to take much of the credit for the job in a Dutch magazine which he thought John wouldn't see in Britain, Jack Stoof has also become a firm friend and it was through Jack that John got involved in the Mannheim stator project.

Other notable heavy loads shifted during this period included a pair of

John Wynn, with his back to the camera, walks alongside the trailer as the crew inspect the damaged kerbstones. The loaded trailer weighs more than 220 tons in all.

230-ton Bessemer converter shells, together with their 245-ton trunnion rings, which were off-loaded from a heavy lift ship at Port Talbot and delivered to the British Steel Margam plant in June 1968.

In 1970, in a similar operation, three 253-ton furnaces manufactured by Head Wrightson Process Engineering were brought to a specially-constructed deep berth at Newport Deeps in the Bristol Channel where they were rolled onto seven-line trailers for road delivery to Llanwern. Each of the three deliveries also included a trunnion ring.

Two years later, in 1972, a number of huge vessel sections manufactured by Whessoe of Darlington were conveyed from Swansea Docks to the Lummus Company's site at BP Chemicals, Baglan Bay and to the National Oil Refinery at Llandarcy.

In what must have been a glorious sight, four Contractors and a Pacific were required to move a 220-ton stator, one of six similar units, up the 1:6 Buttrills Hill at Barry, Glamorgan. The stator was being moved from Barry to Aberthaw, having first been brought from the Manchester Docks on the CEGB's *Aberthaw Fisher*, one of a pair of similar vessels, the other being the *Kingsnorth Fisher*. A pair of 15-in naval gun barrels, each weighing 100 tons and mentioned earlier, were transported from Shoeburyness to the Imperial War Museum at Lambeth and were mounted on concrete pedestals. When

construction work on what became the Eurotunnel started on both sides of the Channel in 1974, Wynns delivered the boring machine that started to cut the tunnel from the British side. In January 1975, to the dismay of the French partners, the British Government cancelled the project and the machine was walled-up inside the tunnel until work restarted in 1988.

During this time, Wynns' general transport operations also continued but, sadly there were hard times ahead. The days of Wynns as a family concern had already come to an end but the name was also soon to disappear from everything except the heavy-haulage operation. The economic difficulties which Britain faced at the end of the 1970s led to the closure of Wynns' Newport headquarters and depot – today, the old Shaftesbury Street depot is the site of a huge Sainsbury's supermarket. Most of the vehicles were transferred to a new company based at Stafford, which was formed out of the merger of Wynns and Wrekin Roadways. The new organisation was named Wynns Heavy Haulage of Stafford.

There were to be no Wynns involved in this venture. John resigned in June 1982, frustrated with what he saw as 'big business politics', and his cousin Noel chose to take retirement although he remained involved with the industry, becoming chairman of the Road Haulage Association (RHA), county chairman of the Confederation

of British Industry (CBI), member of the national and Wales councils of the CBI, and a fellow of the Chartered Institute of Logistics and Transport (CILT). John Wynn remained intimately involved with heavy haulage, seemingly unable to escape what was clearly his destiny.

The new Wynns Heavy Haulage operation also acquired at least one, and perhaps two, Contractors (WNT 307S and XFA 217X), which had formerly been the property of Wrekin Roadways. One of these was painted in GEC livery and serviced the remaining contracts from that company's Stafford works. The other eventually passed to Abnormal Load Engineering (ALE) of Hixon, Staffordshire when that company was formed in 1983.

Sadly, the merger did not improve things and the worsening financial position led to the merger of Wynns Heavy Haulage with Sunters of Northallerton to form yet another new organisation, dubbed United Heavy Transport... which did at least retain the distinctive red Wynns livery. Within a year this company had merged with Econofreight to form United Econofreight Heavy Haulage but by 1990, this too had been taken over.

Fortunately, ex-Wynns' Contractors *Renown* (Wynns' fleet number 600, KAX 395P), *Musketeer* (633, YWO 24T) and *Superior* (602, RWO 73R), and perhaps others, have passed into preservation, while other trucks found useful second lives overseas. •

In the 1970s, the Pacific tractor *Dreadnought* (GDW 177) was extensively rebuilt using a Scammell Contractor chassis and other parts, and was re-registered as NDW 345G. Subsequently, Wynns ordered a Contractor without engine and transmission, with the idea of building a custom truck but the work eventually led to Scammell and Wynns designing the Contractor Mk 2.

The 240-ton *Crusader*, with the aid of a 100-ton 'pusher' tractor, crests a small bridge near Windermere with a 105-ton paper cylinder on its way from Beetham, Cumbria. At the end of the journey Wynns was responsible for raising the cylinder 15 feet before sliding it into position.

Wynns Scammell Contractor fleet

Fleet no	Registration no	Date	Name	GTW* and configuration	Notes
182	NDW 836G	1969	*Conqueror*	Mk 1; 240 ton; crew cab, ballast body/fifth wheel	To Sudan
183	JDW 247F	1967	*Traveller*	Mk 1; 150 ton; small cab, ballast body/fifth wheel	To Sudan
184	NDW 837G	1969	*Challenger*	Mk 1; 240 ton; crew cab, ballast body	To Wynns Heavy Haulage
185	JDW 147F	1967	*Adventurer*	Mk 1; 150 ton; small cab, ballast body/fifth-wheel	To Sudan
186	GDW 848E	1967		Mk 1; 100 ton; small cab, ballast body	
187	NDW 838G	1969	*Crusader*	Mk 1; 240 ton; crew cab, ballast body/fifth wheel	To Tanzania, Namibia
188	FDW 769E	1966		Mk 1; 100 ton; small cab, ballast body/fifth wheel	
189	GDW 231D	1966		Mk 1; 100 ton; small cab, ballast body/fifth wheel	
190	GDW 249D	1966		Mk 1; 100 ton; small cab, ballast body	
191	NDW 839H	1969	*Supreme*	Mk 1; 240 ton; crew cab, ballast body	To Tanzania, Namibia
193	RDW 339M	1974	*Hercules*	Mk 1; 240 ton; crew cab, ballast body/fifth wheel	To Tanzania, Namibia
194	SDW 173N	1974	*Champion*	Mk 1; 240 ton; crew cab, ballast body/fifth wheel	To Tanzania, Namibia
195	GTX 211N	1974	*Resolute*	Mk 1; 240 ton; crew cab, ballast body	To Nigeria, then Wynns Heavy Haulage
196	HHB 361N	1974	*Talisman*	Mk 1; 240 ton; crew cab, narrow ballast body	To Sudan
198	SDW 545J	1970		Mk 1; 150 ton; small cab, ballast body	To Nigeria
200	SDW 937J	1970		Mk 1; 150 ton; small cab, ballast body/fifth wheel	
280	TDW 83J	1971		Mk 1; 150 ton; small cab, fifth wheel	To Sudan
281	UDW 139J	1971		Mk 1; 150 ton; small cab, ballast body	To Nigeria
600	KAX 395P	1976	*Renown*	Mk 1; 240 ton; crew cab, ballast body/fifth wheel	To Wynns Heavy Haulage; now preserved
602	RWO 73R	1977	*Superior*	Mk 2; 250 ton; crew cab, narrow ballast body	To Wynns Heavy Haulage, Econofreight; now preserved
604	OBO 3R	1977	*Illustrious*	Mk 1; 240 ton; crew cab, narrow ballast body	To Nigeria
628	XAX 512T	1979	*Cavalier*	Mk 1; 240 ton; crew cab, ballast body	To Wynns Heavy Haulage
631	YAX 165T	1979	*Buccaneer*	Mk 1; 240 ton; crew cab, narrow ballast body	Ex-Wrekin Roadways, to Wynns Heavy Haulage
633	YWO 24T	1979	*Musketeer*	Mk 1; 240 ton; crew cab, ballast body	To Wynns Heavy Haulage, Econofreight; now preserved
640	DBO 661V	1980	*Invincible*	Mk 2; 250 ton; crew cab, narrow ballast body	To Wynns Heavy Haulage
	XFA 217X**	1981	*Dreadnought*	Mk 1; 240 ton; crew cab, ballast body	Finished in GEC livery
	DBF 133Y	1981		Mk 2; 250 ton; crew cab, ballast body	To Econofreight
	DBF 134Y	1981		Mk 2; 250 ton; crew cab, ballast body	To Econofreight

* Gross train weight; these are Scammell's figures and can be considered to be more than conservative.

** XFA 217X was one of two Contractors finished in GEC livery but does not appear in any of the Wynns' fleet records. Since the registration is Staffordshire-based rather than the more usual Newport, it may well have been an ex-Wrekin Roadways vehicle. The name Dreadnought, of course, was originally used on Pacific number 192 (GDW 277).

Above Subsequently named *Dreadnought*, Pacific tractor GDW 277 (fleet number 192) looks magnificent in its brand-new red and black livery. The trailer is number 333, a 130-ton Cranes unit and is loaded with a huge English Electric transformer. As is so often the case, a Scammell brings up the rear.

Dreadnought again. This time the transformer is being carried on the 200-ton 24-wheeled trailer numbered 444, which was developed from the 130-ton trailer number 333.

Flashback....

Export or die!

Over the years, Wynns' expertise in moving oversized and difficult loads became legendary, and word of the company's abilities began to spread around the world. Not surprisingly, this was followed by requests to become involved in overseas' operations, with the first such project coming in the late 1950s when the company supplied three Diamond T tractors and trailers to Spain, and helped to train Spanish crews to move three large generators.

In 1959, Arthur Matthews went to Argentina to supervise the movement and installation of heavy equipment, and trailer number 555 was sold to the company who had commissioned the consultancy. Other contracts followed, notably for the delivery of oil-refinery equipment in Cyprus, when the Pacific tractor *Helpmate* (Wynns' fleet number 196, GDW 585) was shipped to the island together with a suitable trailer.

Plenty more overseas' work followed over the next decades.

During the 1960s, the civil-engineering company Balfour Beattie was the senior consultant in the construction of the Niger Dam at Kainji in Nigeria. The scheme involved harnessing river rapids near Bussa,

with the dam creating a lake that would supply hydro-electric power sufficient for almost half of Nigeria's requirements. Percy Wynn ('HP') had been invited by Balfour Beattie to advise on how the equipment might be moved... and his visit to Nigeria was on the very day that the country's independence was announced.

Unfortunately, the River Niger was un-navigable and it was obvious that the massive transformers would have to be moved by a combination of road and rail from Apapa Port, Lagos to Kainji. This involved the construction of

a new road from the railhead at Mokwa to the dam site 70 miles away, and the design of a special transporter.

'HP' recommended that Head Wrightson of Thornaby, and Cranes of Dereham work together on the design of the unique, and hugely impressive, road/rail transporter (RRT) which was subsequently dubbed the 'Yellow Peril' by Wynns' staff who worked with it in Africa. The RRT carried the transformers in a cradle that could be mounted on either road or rail bogies, conversion from one mode to the other being facilitated by hydraulic support

One of Mammoet's Mack 895 tractors poses between the two 240-ton Contractors, *Crusader* and *Champion*. The trucks carried equipment 1,500 miles, from Tanzania to Zambia.

Painted in the distinctive Wynns' red with a black ballast box, and carrying a large transformer on a pair of four-line bogies, *Crusader* heads up the convoy travelling between Mombasa and Gtaru. The dusty road and inevitable Peugeot leave no doubt that this is Africa.

With *Hercules* coupled to a swan-neck trailer, John Wynn explains the route to some of the locally-recruited crew before the load sets out from Dar-es-Salaam for the Kariba North Power Station.

During a break in the loading procedure, some of the Nigerian crew find respite from the sun under the 'Yellow Peril' – the Crane Fruehauf designed road/rail transporter (RRT) used to carry the transformers... clearly no 'health and safety' concerns here!

150-ton Contractor, owned by the Niger Dam Authority and resplendent in its yellow livery, coupled to the road/rail transporter (RRT). The transformers were carried in a cradle which could be mounted on either road or rail bogies.

legs. Two 150-ton Scammell Contractors were purchased by the Niger Dam Authority and, after a period of trials with the RRT in Britain, the tractors and the transporter were shipped to Nigeria. In 1967, Rex Evans travelled to Nigeria to supervise the assembly of the RRT at Lagos docks and to undertake the training of the Italian and Nigerian crews using a mock-up of the transformer. He also used the rig on a proving run to satisfy the Nigerian rail authorities that the project was feasible. After supervising the movement of the first 120-ton transformer from Lagos to Kainji, Rex returned to Britain, leaving the main contractor to deal with the three remaining units.

Four years later, Noel Wynn was in Nigeria discussing the possibility of moving two 140-ton transformers from Apapa to Onitsha and Oshogbo using combinations of barge and road in the first case, and road and rail in the second. The two 150-ton Scammell tractors, now owned by the National Electric Power Authority (NEPA) of Nigeria and registered locally as LN 8144 and LN 8145, were pressed into service again, as was the RRT trailer. At Onitsha the offloading operation was

particularly tricky since the barge was unable to approach the ramp head on due to a combination of low water level and the presence of a sunken ferry. The latter, which the authorities had failed to disclose to Noel during his 'recce' for

the project, was a casualty of the Biafran War.

Within a year, Wynns was over on the other side of the world, shipping what were effectively palletised loads to the USA and Canada via Atlantic

Container Lines... on one occasion travelling on the ill-fated *Atlantic Conveyor* vessel which was sunk during the Falklands War. One load, destined for Allis Chalmers in Pennsylvania, was loaded onto a Cranes trailer in Britain and then hauled to Liverpool by one of Wynns' Scammell Contractors where it was pushed onto the ship... at Newport News, Virginia, Wynns' partners, Lockwood Brothers, pulled the trailer off the ship with their own tractor and completed the delivery without any need to unload the trailer.

More intriguing were a number of similar trans-Atlantic jobs which entailed delivering over-size loads and, at the same time, shipping a Diamond T tractor (Wynns' fleet number 199, HDW 107) which had been converted to a fifth-wheel tractor. The Diamond T was used to finish the delivery at the other end of the sea voyage. Only Wynns could have contemplated repatriating a Diamond T to its country of origin following its original military service and a full working life in Britain.

Rex Evans made more visits to Nigeria between 1972 and 1974, when Mitsubishi Electric contracted Wynns to move 18 140-ton transformers to almost a dozen different locations across the country. Once again, the moves involved a combination of road/rail and road/barge techniques, with the RRT proving its value yet again. Associated Portland Cement Manufacturers also employed Wynns to move 20,000 tons of machinery for a number of cement plants across Nigeria. The contract was expected to last six years, with road movements only allowed on Sundays, often across unfinished roads. Tractors, trailers and personnel were brought from Britain; for example, *Illustrious* (Wynns' fleet number 604, OBO 3R), one of the 240-ton Scammell Contractors, was shipped to Nigeria 'brand new' for this job, as was *Resolute* (195, GTX 211N), the latter fitted with an experimental torque-converter transmission.

Nearer home, John had received a request for assistance from Jack Stoof. Whilst with Stoof Transport in the Netherlands, Jack had helped Wynns with the supply of the three sets of double-width bogies which were used to move the three large vessels from Birkenhead to the Shell refinery at Stanlow back in 1971. At the time these were the largest loads ever to have been moved on British roads. However, Jack had left Stoof Transport and had started his own heavy-haulage company which he had named Infra Transport.

Jack wanted John to assist Infra Transport to move a 460-ton stator from Mannheim in Germany to the

In Tanzania it was not uncommon to come across sections of road that had collapsed. Tommy Cromwell navigates *Crusader* around a local Fiat tanker, hoping that the remaining surface will support the weight of the truck and trailer.

Netherlands. Whilst Infra Transport were in the habit of running trailers side by side to accommodate excess width, it seems that Wynns 19ft-wide Nicolas bogies were perfect for this particular job because the access doorway at the end of the haul was just 236 inches wide – a pair of Infra Transport's trailers would have been around 4ins too wide to make the final delivery! Infra Transport also provided the motive power for the project in the form of a powerful Dutch-built FTF tractor. John had flown to Dar-es-Salaam with Henk Van Wezel to start the Zambian job, and 'HP' and Rex Evans went to the off-loading site in the Netherlands where 'HP' was very unhappy at the way Wynns' name was associated with what he saw as a hotch-potch of tractors and equipment that were being used on the job.

The year 1973 saw a pair of Wynns' Contractors in France where the company had undertaken to move a pair of enormous cylindrical steel struts which had been manufactured by Babcock Atlantique at St Nazaire, and

which were destined for a North Sea oil platform at Graythorpe, near Hartlepool; the larger of the two struts weighed 196 tons and measured up at 144 feet in length and 20 feet in diameter. John and Rex Evans drove to St Nazaire to look after the project, and the move required the struts to be loaded onto a roll on/roll off (RoRo) vessel at St Nazaire and then offloaded in Britain and moved seven miles from the dock to Laing's at Graythorpe where the rig was being assembled. The move was effected by a pair of 240-ton Contractors together with two seven-row multi-wheel Nicolas bogie sets.

A year or so later, in 1974/75, Wynns undertook what was certainly its largest overseas project to date when the company was contracted to move turbine and electrical equipment to the Kariba North Power Station in southern Zambia. What should have been a relatively straightforward project was made more complicated by Ian Smith's 1965 Unilateral Declaration of Independence (UDI) in the former

The Mammoet crews were disappointed to discover that their Mack 895 tractors were no match for Wynns' mighty Contractors particularly through the Kitonga Gorge in what is now the Udzungwa Mountains National Park in the Southern Highlands of Tanzania.

With some assistance from the rear, *Hercules* hauls another piece of equipment destined for the Kariba North Power Station.

British colony of Rhodesia – now Zimbabwe. The dam was located on the Zambezi river close to the Zambia/Rhodesia border but sanctions imposed on Smith's regime meant that it was not possible to bring the trucks up by road through South Africa and Rhodesia, and John Wynn and Rex

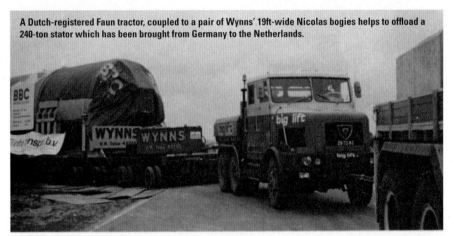

A Dutch-registered Faun tractor, coupled to a pair of Wynns' 19ft-wide Nicolas bogies helps to offload a 240-ton stator which has been brought from Germany to the Netherlands.

Another view of the 240-ton BBC stator as it is brought up a slight incline at the off-loading site.

Evans flew out to Lusaka with the idea of scouting alternative routes.

Checking bridges on the route, the pair were surprised to find themselves under surveillance, and more, by the Tanzanian Army who considered that they might be terrorists! John Wynn recalled that it was a sobering experience to find himself looking down the business end of rifle being held by a frightened 18-year old! It was established that the equipment could be off-loaded at Dar-es-Salaam in Tanzania and then transported 1,500 miles west to the dam site. A holding area was established at Kafue sidings, south of Lusaka, and around 100 miles from the dam. Equipment was to be offloaded here and held until required by the Yugoslav team constructing the dam.

The contract involved more than 3,000 tons of equipment and, believing this to be too much for Wynns acting alone, the company agreed to join forces with the Dutch company Mammoet who would supply three 150-ton trailers, three American-made Mack 895 tractors and one Dutch-built FTF tractor; Mammoet also agreed to provide a fully-equipped mobile workshop, refueling facilities… and a shower! For their part, Wynns brought along a double-neck swan trailer (Wynns' fleet number 654) to handle the transformers, two 150-ton trailers and four 240-ton Scammell Contractors, two of which were brand new. There was also a caravan of six Ford Transit motor homes that provided air-conditioned sleeping facilities for the drivers and

John Wynn poses in front of one of the Mack 895 tractors operated by the Dutch Mammoet concern. The Macks had a higher top speed than the Contractors but John was not impressed with the overall performance of the tractor.

crew, albeit the air-conditioning units were so noisy as to make sleep all but impossible. Three of the Transits were allocated to the Dutch crews and three to Wynns, and the vehicles were all painted in different colours to make recognition easy. The Wynns' crews also included Sunters' personnel since both were now part of the United Transport Group. Escort and night security services were provided for the convoys by the Tanzanian Army and Police Service travelling in Land Rovers, or on motorcycles alongside the trucks. The Tanzanian escort would erect three large bundles of undergrowth at the front and rear of the convoy whenever it was parked for the night, giving on-coming traffic three chances of stopping before hitting the vehicles!

The convoy speed was deliberately held down to around 10mph, which meant that little more than 70 miles could be covered each day, with the trucks starting out around 6.00am and staying on the road until early afternoon when the temperature often reached 100°F. Much to the chagrin of the Dutch crews who believed that the superior turn of speed of the Macks gave them an advantage, the Scammells quickly proved themselves to be the better machine, particularly on the most challenging part of the job through the Kitonga Gorge in what is now the Udzungwa Mountains National Park in the Southern Highlands of Tanzania. The section involved a five-mile climb with gradients up to 1:10 and, whilst it required all three of Mammoet's Mack tractors to climb through the gorge with a 60-ton stator, Wynns could manage the same load with just two Scammells. Just to keep things interesting, there was a half-mile tunnel at the dam site leading to the underground off-loading bay and it needed two tractors to negotiate this

The Pacific tractor *Helpmate* was shipped to Cyprus in November 1970 where it was used to deliver equipment for an oil refinery at Larnaca. After the contract, the truck stayed on the island and was painted grey.

Crusader gets a new coat of paint – red on the cab for Wynns, and black on the ballast box to reflect the interests of Express Kenya... again, note the casual attitude towards occupational health and safety shown by the workers.

Kariba North Power Station again, and a pair of Wynns' Contractors negotiate a Mammoet trailer into the half-mile tunnel at the dam site leading to the underground off-loading bay. The rear tractor is going to act as a brake as the load descends into the tunnel.

section, one pulling, while the other acted as a brake to prevent the load running away.

At the end of the project, the two newer Contractors were returned to Britain whilst the older tractors were shipped to Kenya together with three trailers and were repainted at the premises of Express Kenya in Nairobi. The cabs were finished in the familiar Wynns' red, whilst the ballast boxes were painted in Express Kenya's colours since the two companies were collaborating on a contract to transport of a pair of 75-ton transformers from Mombasa to Gtaru, a distance of 400 miles across the Kenyan plains. The transformers had to be carried higher than normal in the trailer frames in order to provide increased ground clearance and, at the end of the journey, the crews had to carefully negotiate the load down the partially-constructed dam wall into the substation.

In 1977, Wynns became involved in a huge project in Sudan, transporting 3,000 tons of equipment for the construction of a sugar refinery across 1,400 miles of largely unmade road. So large was this project that it requires a chapter all to itself but, before we take a look at that incredible undertaking, it is worth looking at the 1980 operation in Ghana when Wynns moved ten large-diameter kiln sections and other equipment from Takoradi to Nsuta. The equipment was destined for the production of manganese nodules at an open-cast mine at Nsuta. Two new Scammell Crusader ballast tractors were purchased by Taysec, a Ghanaian operation run by Taylor Woodrow, together with an unusual six-row steerable Nicolas trailer on which the axles were spaced 15 feet apart to keep the axle loading below 15 tons. With the platform trailer height at 58 inches to provide ground clearance, there were inevitable stability problems and this

led to some modifications being made to the suspension layout once the kiln sections were loaded. Conditions on the route were such that it was often necessary for the tractors to be double-headed which necessitated the crews synchronising gear changes by a system of hand signals.

Still in the 1970s, but away from Africa, Wynns became involved in the construction of power stations in Israel. The Israel Electric Corporation (IEC) had sought advice on design and construction from the British Central Electricity Generating Board (CEGB) and, since there were no Israeli heavy-haulage contractors capable of undertaking delivery of the equipment from the port to the construction site, had also enquired about this aspect of the job. The CEGB suggested that Wynns and Pickfords be approached but the work went to Wynns since the IEC was reluctant to deal with what was still a nationalised company. Equipment was being supplied by Britain, the USA and Canada, and the contract involved loading Parsons' transformers onto a RoRo ship in Britain, then travelling to Malta where the ship took on US-built generators and Canadian boilers. At Ashod Port, south of Tel Aviv, Wynns unloaded the equipment and delivered it to the power station site.

A subsequent contract for a power station midway between Haifa and Tel Aviv saw Wynns also becoming involved in the design of the equipment itself, just to ensure that it could be carried on the company's largest trailer, number 999. Fears of a Middle East boycott against Wynns if the company continued to work in Israel eventually saw the trailer sold to a middle man, John Silbermann of Hallet, who subcontracted the work direct to Wynns personnel to enable the project to be completed.

One of the last of Wynns' overseas contracts was on the Marshall Islands in the Pacific where four 46-ton engines and 30-ton alternators were exported to Majuro. The work was contracted to Transtec but with the stipulation that the actual movement of the equipment on site was undertaken by Wynns' personnel. Wynns was thus sub-contracted to Transtec, and Pete Collier and Bernard James went over to the Marshall Islands for the job. The same pair also installed generator sets on the Pacific islands of Guam and Guadalcanal, and in the Philippines.

And finally, in 1983, Wynns trailer 304 was used to deliver a number of boilers from Natal to Tutuka and Majuba. A local heavy-haulage contractor undertook the final delivery, and in total ignorance of the significance of the Pacific tractors in Wynns' history, coupled the Wynns trailer to a modern Pacific tractor. •

John Wynn poses, with Austin 1100, in front of *Helpmate* soon after the tractor was exported to Cyprus.

The Kenana Sugar Company

Bedford were so pleased with Wynns' verdict on the performance of their TM trucks in Sudan that the company used this picture in its advertisement in the trade press.

At the end of 1977, Wynns undertook what proved to be their most difficult overseas operation to date, transporting a huge amount of equipment for the construction of a refinery for the newly-formed Kenana Sugar Company Limited in Sudan.

The refinery in question was a joint project between the Sudanese Government and the British conglomerate Lonhro, which had been operating in Africa since 1909, initially as the London and Rhodesian Mining and Land Company. Since 1961, Lonhro had been under the chairmanship of 'Tiny' Rowland – the man for whom, incidentally, the phrase 'the unacceptable face of capitalism' was coined – and Rowland had transformed the company into a worldwide conglomerate. In 1977, Lonhro turned over £1,257 million, of which £653 million was earned in sub-Saharan Africa. Profits stood at £90 million. At its peak in 1989, Lonhro's profits were £272 million, up from a mere £158,000 in 1961.

Lonhro had entered into an agreement with the Sudanese Government in 1972 to construct a major sugar plantation and processing facility at Rabak, 200 miles south-east of Khartoum. The company's initial stake in the project was 12.5 per cent but, in 1976, this was reduced to 5.5 per cent, with Lonhro's management agreement terminated in 1977. However, within 12 months Lonhro's involvement in the project had been favourably renegotiated with the company now owning 3.36 per cent of a project with a much larger equity base. The company was also paid a compensation fee of $1.5 million for the termination of the management agreement.

Independent since 1956, the Republic of Sudan is the largest country in Africa, and the tenth largest in the world, with an area of almost one million square miles. The country shares borders with Egypt, Eritrea, Ethiopia, Kenya, Uganda, the Congo, the Central African Republic, Chad and Libya. It is dominated by the River Nile and its tributaries, and the terrain consists generally of flat plains, broken by mountain ranges. The climate is equatorial, with a rainy season which lasts for about three months during July and September in the north, and up to six months – June to November – in the south. The level of rainfall increases towards the south, where there are swamps and rainforest. In the capital, Khartoum, average annual rainfall varies from more than 6 inches to around 39 inches, with most occurring between April and October.

Champion dwarfs the Bedford MK used as a 'chuck wagon' in Sudan.

Average temperatures in Khartoum range from 60 to 90°F in January, to a staggering 110°F in June.

For Wynns, the project had begun in early 1977 when John had flown to Sudan at the request of John Temme, Logistics Manager for the Kenana Sugar Company. John Temme had been visiting his parents in Newport in late 1976, and had talked to his father – who was the Chief Engineer of Newport Borough Council and knew Wynns well – about the problems he faced in getting the equipment for the new refinery from Port Sudan on the Red Sea coast, to Rabak, south of the Sudanese capital Khartoum. His father had suggested that Wynns might have the expertise to be able to undertake the job and John Temme immediately made contact with John Wynn. The two men met to discuss the project and, within days, John Wynn was on his way to Sudan to inspect the port facilities and to survey the conditions along possible routes.

There was a total of 3,000 tons of equipment for the plant, which was to be moved in self-sufficient convoys, each consisting of six trucks carrying 180-200-tons between them, accompanied by fuel and water, living quarters, and road-making, workshop and cooking facilities. The distance between the port and the plant site was little more than 550 miles as the crow flies but each convoy had an actual round-trip distance of 1,350 miles in temperatures up to 110°F... and the whole contract was to be completed in a total just 179 days. It was to be quite a challenge!

Starting at the docks in the north-eastern city of Port Sudan, the convoys would move inland, travelling south-west to Rabak in the White Nile Province, about 150 miles south of Khartoum. Although this meant that the journey would start out in the arid north, fortunately it would not be necessary to spend much time in the Nubian Desert, where sand storms, known locally as haboob, can completely block out the sun.

However, clearly, working in Sudan was going to present its particular set of problems, not least of which was that the contract would have to be scheduled to avoid the rainy months. And, having seen the queues at filling

Not your average jaunt down the M6!

The convoy was crossing some of the most desolate country on the planet and the convoys were designed to be self-sufficient. Water and fuels, particularly, were a scarce and valuable commodity... the former for both the trucks and the crews and several trailers were fitted with 800-gallon auxiliary tanks on the swan-neck.

stations, John rightly identified that the provision of adequate fuel supplies would also be something of a challenge. When Wynns submitted their quotation for the project on 26 January 1977, it included the proviso that supplying fuel for the convoys would be the responsibility of Kenana.

The standard of the roads in Sudan was also cause for concern and it was a further condition of the contract that Kenana provide a Caterpillar 16G six-wheeled motorised grader which would accompany the convoy. John was well aware of the capabilities of the big 'Cat' having seen one in action when Wynns

were delivering 60-ton sections of a Ransomes & Rapier 1800 'walker' at Maesgwyn in South Wales. The grader was self-propelled and did not require its own transport. Although it was slow, it could easily keep up with the convoy and could also be used to assist the vehicles through soft or otherwise difficult conditions, as well as being used to repair damaged or impassable sections of road. As regards food, technical support and accommodation, the convoys were designed to be self-sufficient, but a light aircraft was always on hand to assist in the event of an emergency. A number of trucks in

the convoy were painted with the word 'Wynns', writ large on their white-painted roofs to aid recognition from the air.

On 17 April 1977, Wynns received confirmation that they had been awarded the contract and the company started to prepare the vehicles that would be required.

Three 240-ton Scammell Contractors (*Conqueror*, *Hercules* and *Champion*, Wynns' fleet numbers 182, 193 and 194, respectively) were overhauled in the company's Newport workshops, having the ballast bodies removed to convert them to fifth-wheel

The Caterpillar wheeled grader proved invaluable for repairing bad sections of road, and for dragging the loaded trucks out of the soft sand or up steep inclines.

Hercules and *Champion* side-by-side in Wynns' workshop being prepared for the Sudan contract, having been converted from ballast-box to fifth-wheel configuration.

Below: One of the drop-frame trailers which was fitted with an 800-gallon tank for fuel or water.

John Wynn takes the keys to the Bedford TM. While the TM was not Wynns' first choice as a support vehicle, it more than proved itself under very difficult conditions.

configuration, as well as being fitted with substantial sump guards. Both *Hercules* and *Champion* had recently returned from their spell in Tanzania and, following the conversion work, were destined to return, almost immediately, to Africa! Resplendent in newly-applied red, black and white paint, and bearing the name Wynns together with specially-designed decals describing the contract, the three tractors were also decorated with the British and Sudanese flags on the bumpers and cab roofs.

Smaller tractors were also required for support, and three new Bedford TM 6x4 tractors, powered by Detroit Diesel 8V-71 engines, were purchased. Although they were never registered in Britain, the trucks were named *Diamond*, *Emerald* and *Sapphire*, and allocated Wynns' fleet numbers 609, 610, 611. The convoy was completed by the addition of two new 4x4 Bedford KMs, one of which (608) was equipped with a Hiab hydraulic crane and workshop body, the other (612) being fitted with refrigeration units and fitted out as a 'chuck wagon'. It is interesting to note that Bedford was not the company's first choice; Wynns would almost certainly have preferred to buy Foden, Atkinson or ERF trucks, but none of these were available – Bedford was the only British truck company that was able to offer suitable trucks 'off the shelf'. As it turned out, there was no need for any misgivings since the Luton trucks proved themselves more than

Land Rovers were not easily available in Britain in 1977 and this long-wheelbase pick-up, one of two acquired for the project, came from Kenya in 'knocked-down' form.

capable of what was demanded of them even under the harsh conditions prevailing in Sudan, a fact which Bedford exploited in contemporary advertising material.

The eight trucks, together with three dollies and six two-, three- and four-axle drop-frame semi-trailers, some of the latter fitted with 800-gallon auxiliary fuel and water tanks on the swan-neck above the fifth wheel coupling, were shipped to Port Sudan on Sudan Line's MV *Nyala* from Workington. Two new long-wheelbase Series 3 Land Rovers, at the time virtually unobtainable in Britain within a reasonable timescale, were purchased through John's friend Dave Edwards in Kenya in 'knocked-down'

form and were assembled by Express Kenya. The Land Rovers were subsequently shipped to Port Sudan as support vehicles, arriving on 10 November 1977, just two days before the first convoy set out for Rabak.

Also on 10 November, the Wynns' trucks and equipment arrived at Port Sudan and, with little time wasted, the first convoy set out from Port Sudan two days later, with John Wynn himself frequently taking a turn at driving one of the Contractors. For part of the journey the convoy was accompanied by Bedford fuel tankers which had been provided by Kenana, whilst drinking water was obtained from local wells, often being brought to the convoy by donkey!

When not carrying a load, the two drop-frame trailers could be carried together. Here, we see one trailer being loaded onto the other.

At the time, the road between Port Sudan and Khartoum, the capital of Sudan, was still under construction but even allowing for this, the going was never easy. Whilst there were properly-surfaced sections, the mixture of mountain and desert terrain was a challenge for both men and machines and the trucks were also occasionally required to ford rivers where there were no proper crossing facilities. It was also common to come across overturned local trucks on the highway sections where the Sudanese drivers had fallen asleep at the wheel, or where mechanical failure had caused a runaway accident. However, the Caterpillar grader more than proved its worth, despite Kenana's oversight in not providing a driver – an omission ably rectified by Wynns' Peter Milne, and providing a nice little extra source of income for the company! The huge six-wheeled machine was frequently called upon to drag the loaded trucks out of the soft sand or up steep inclines and, with plenty of off-road sections to negotiate, the 16-foot 'dozer blade was more than capable of a little on-the-spot road-making, on one occasion even building an impromptu railway crossing.

The first convoy arrived at its destination on 19 December, five weeks after leaving Port Sudan, having averaged a little under 40 miles a day. Whilst this might seem like slow progress, remember, the heat of the

At the time, the 4x4 Bedford MK was the British Army's standard workhorse in the 4-ton class so there were few doubts that this vehicle would be suitable for the heavy going in Sudan.

day meant that operations had to cease in early afternoon when the temperature could reach 110°F.

Always reluctant to run empty, on the return journey John actually managed to find a couple of Ruston-Bucyrus 22RB crawler cranes to back load to Khartoum on behalf of Alfred McAlpine. They had been in use during the early construction phases at the Kenana site but, with their tasks completed, had become surplus to requirements.

Back at Port Sudan, the second convoy was assembled and this process continued until the last load was delivered to Rabak on 10 May 1978. Despite the heat and dust, all of the vehicles acquitted themselves extremely well. The Wynns' crews had come to expect reliability from the

mighty Scammells, but the TM 6x4s also performed extremely well.

The Kenana Sugar Company continues in business to this day, claiming to be the 'world's largest integrated sugar company'. The Kenana estate covers 84,078 acres and the factory is designed to process 17,000 tons of sugar cane daily, producing around 330,000 tons of white sugar a year aimed, essentially, at export markets. The plant is ideally situated on the eastern bank of the White Nile, less than 150 miles south of Sudan's capital, Khartoum. Here, the rich alluvial soils of the Blue Nile flood plain are ideal for the cultivation of sugar cane and production of sugar at Kenana has increased steadily from 100,000 tons in 1980/81 when the plant opened, with the 300,000 ton rated design capacity of the plant surpassed for the first time in 1984/5 – a tribute to the skill and industry of the workforce and the expertise of the Wynns team and the products of Scammell and Bedford. In the autumn of 2009, in response to the rising price of sugar, Kenana announced that it was planning to more than triple sugar output within three years. New plant under construction will take output to more than three million tons from the current level of 900,000 tons. The company has also diversified in recent years and other products include animal feeds, molasses, dairy products, timber, woodchips and paper pulp, as well as agricultural tools and equipment. •

The two flat-topped bogie units could also easily be carried stacked two-high for the return trip.

Flashback...

Pacific *Dreadnought*, with support from one of the ex-WD Scammell Pioneers, carries a huge chemical vessel on a pair of four-line solid-tyred bogies.

The Sudan-Ren fer plant

One of the two 83-ton corner-tube units crossing a concrete bridge *en-route* to Khartoum. The tractor is *Talisman*, one of Wynns' 240-ton Scammell Contractors.

Although it was the first time that Wynns had worked in the challenging conditions which prevailed in Sudan, the Kenana Sugar Company project had not been the company's first foray into Africa... and it would not be the last. Following the completion of the last leg of the Kenana project in May 1978, there was a period when the Wynns' trucks undertook some local 'spot' projects, involving moving boats, brewing vats and bulldozers.

However, the expertise which the company had shown in completing the Kenana contract run soon led to involvement in a new project. Polytra NV, a Belgian transport engineering and logistics company, was the lead transport contractor involved in the construction of the state-owned Sudan-Ren fertiliser plant at Khartoum. Wynns were asked by Polytra to help shift over-sized equipment to the plant, including five cylindrical storage vessels and a pair of massive Borsig corner-tube boilers.

Of the smaller trucks which had been purchased for the Kenana project, one of the Bedford TMs, which was effectively worn out, was sold locally and replaced by a 6x4 Atkinson Venturer. A second-hand Lima motorised crane was purchased from Southern Counties of Portsmouth, and refurbished in Wynns' Newport workshops before being shipped to Sudan where it was used to assist in loading and unloading the heavy equipment. A small Fordson agricultural tractor was also acquired for use as a shunter, and Sudan-Ren themselves provided a 120-ton Coles motorised crane which was intended for off-loading at the construction site. The crane also accompanied one of the convoys where it was 'looked after' by Wynns en-route to Khartoum. Unfortunately, it was out of its depth in the rough terrain and the condition of the roads meant that the crane frequently needed 'helping out'.

More trucks, trailers and equipment were also shipped to Sudan for the project. With the addition of the 240-ton Contractor *Talisman* (Wynns' fleet number 196, HHB 361N) equipped as a ballast tractor, and 150-ton Contractors *Traveller* (183, JDW 247F), *Adventurer* (185, JDW 147F) and the un-named

tiliser

The load was carried on L36/38, an eight-line flat-top trailer unit, the wheel sets having been taken from Wynns' trailer number 789. John Dixon rode shotgun to control the hydraulics.

What a bizarre sight this must have been to the locals, many of whom were more used to donkeys than motor traffic, let alone outsized loads such as this.

280, all of which had been converted to fifth-wheel configuration, there was a period when Wynns were operating nine Contractors in Africa... almost certainly the largest fleet of heavy Scammells on the continent. Additional trailers included a couple of ex-military Cranes FV3601 50-ton multi-axle tank-transporter units, which proved useful in shifting a huge Caterpillar D8 'dozer, as well as a pair of Cranes four-axle flat-top trailers, originally part of the six-axle bogies of trailer 789 before the company purchased single six-axle bogies. These four-axle units could be linked together to provide an eight-axle unit.

One of the most demanding loads of the contract were the corner-tube boilers, each of which weighed 83 tons and measured 27 feet in height. Carried on a

Much of the route was absolutely desolate but the job could not have been completed without the benefit of the new highway.

The load had to be carried with a distinct offset to the left which meant that it required a degree of skill from John Dixon to maintain its level on the strongly-cambered sections of the highway.

A little local traffic!

It was a long slog up the Aqabar Pass outside of Port Sudan.

Cranes eight-axle flat-top trailer, each boiler towered above the tractor, whilst the offset centre of gravity meant that the load was hanging off one side of the trailer by as much as four feet. Tom Davies took the wheel of *Talisman* and John Dixon rode shotgun on the trailer for the entire run, steering the trailer and controlling the hydraulics which kept the load upright across some very difficult road conditions, including extreme cambers… aside from the loneliness of being alone at the back of the convoy, this was no small feat and required absolute concentration for mile after mile. The height of the load caused particular problems in the city of Khartoum, where overhead cables had to be raised to allow the boiler to pass underneath. Equally challenging in their own way were the five 85-ton bullet-shaped storage vessels, 120-feet long and 11 feet in diameter. Each was carried on the same type of Cranes trailer as the boilers, but this time running as a pair of separate four-axle bolster sets.

During the period of the Kenana Sugar contract, the sole highway between Port Sudan and Khartoum was still under construction and the Wynns' convoys were frequently slowed by the difficulties involved in just negotiating the terrain. The highway was being constructed under five contracts, with each section measuring around 225 miles. It was a real multi-national effort. The first section was constructed by German contractors, the second by Italians, the third by Yugoslavs, the fourth by the Chinese, and the final section by Americans. As time went on, and more of the highway was completed, each of the Kenana journies had entailed less desert mileage but, by the time the Sudan-Ren convoys got underway, the entire 760-mile highway from Port Sudan to Khartoum had been completed. In fact, despite being able to employ a hydraulically-suspended trailer which allowed the load to be maintained on a level keel, John Wynn knows that it would have been impossible to deliver the two enormous corner-tube boilers and the five 120-foot long storage vessels without the completion of the metalled road.

There is no doubt that this was a demanding project, taking its toll on both men and machines and, although the Scammells proved themselves exceptionally reliable, the extreme heat and dust of the Sudan quickly began to have an effect on their appearance. After a few months exposure to the harsh sun, the men began to resemble Californian beach bums, and the once-resplendent gleaming red paint on the trucks became faded and scuffed. Uncle Percy would not have approved!

A steersman's life can be very lonely.

This view shows the four-foot offset of the load.

More 'spot' work was also undertaken in Sudan during the Sudan-Ren contract, including a truck-mounted crane, a JCB excavator, two 75-ton dockside cranes which were moved half a mile within the Port Sudan docks… and, most notably, a 75-ton NCK crawler crane which was moved 725 miles from Port Sudan to Burri Power Station at Khartoum for machinery erectors Capper Neil International. Although the body of the crane was generally carried on one trailer, with the jib and other components on another, for at least one part of the journey the load was hauled, road-train style, on a pair of trailers coupled together and headed by a single Scammell 240-ton tractor – as the company themselves used to say, 'There's a Scammell for every type of load'… and indeed there was!

No sooner was the Sudan-Ren project out of the way than Polytra asked Wynns to join a massive convoy which was transporting equipment to a huge factory site in Nyala, the largest city in South Darfur and possibly the largest industrial town in Sudan, deep in the oil-rich west of the country. The work was being carried out for Held & Francke, an Austrian company which was undertaking groundworks and constructing roadways at the factory complex. This project saw Wynns providing a pair of 240-ton Scammell Contractors, *Conqueror* (Wynns' fleet number 183, NDW 836G) and *Hercules* (193, RDW 339M), as part of a massive 50-vehicle one-off convoy hauling

The corner tubes were hauled 760 miles all the way from Port Sudan to Khartoum.

Talisman was the only one of the Contractors used on the project to retain its original ballast-body configuration.

Champion and *Talisman* pose alongside the Coles 120-ton mobile crane provided by Sudan-Ren for off-loading at the construction site.

trucks, dumpers and other plant and equipment southwest of Khartoum and south of the Darfur region. Although there was a rail link between Khartoum and Nyala it was not suitable for moving the heavy and out-of-gauge loads in question and since there was no proper road, the convoy ran on what were little more than Jeep tracks across more than 400 miles of desert and characteristic African scrubland.

The Wynns' trucks were accompanied by the Bedford KM 'chuck wagon' which had already done sterling service on the Sudan-Ren contract, and a long-wheelbase Land Rover. Wynns' contribution to the exercise was to carry two massive Broyt hydraulic shovels, one older X4 and one X41, loaded on three-axle step-frame semi-trailers, which were coupled to the two Contractors. For their part, Held &

Talisman coupled to an ex-WD 40-ton tank-transporter trailer which is carrying a Caterpillar D8 'dozer.

The Cat' D8 'dozer was carried without its tracks which made it very difficult to move unless the crane was at hand.

The loose sand on large parts of the route meant that the going was never easy.

Held & Francke operated a fleet of MAN 6x4 trucks, equipped as tankers, tractors and tippers.

Water and fuel storage tanks were carried on the Contractors, attached to the trailer swan neck.

Francke deployed a fleet of MAN 6x4 tankers, tractors and tippers, the latter often hauling trailers, which were carrying rock-crushing plant, spare tyres for the wheeled equipment, and the smaller items of plant. Running under their own power, the convoy also included a fleet of brand-new Euclid scow-ended dump trucks.

For most of the route the going was atrocious, with frequent obstacles that included soft sand, narrow bridges, and dry gulleys. It was also frequently necessary to unload one of the Caterpillar 'dozers or graders being carried by one of the other contractors to help extricate trucks which had become bogged down in the sand, sometimes even including the Wynns' Contractors which, remember, with their undriven front axles did not have the benefit of all-wheel drive. Worse still, the heat was such that it was only possible to travel from first light until early afternoon before the daytime sun became unbearable.

Although other commitments forced him to return to Britain before the contract was completed, John was a vital member of the convoy crew, taking a hand at driving and the inevitable digging out, as well as acting as banksman as the outfits picked their way through narrow ravines and gulleys.

Of the trucks used on the project, most were disposed of locally, including the Atkinson and the Scammell Contractors *Conqueror* (Wynns' fleet number 183, NDW 836G), *Traveller* (183, JDW 247F), and the un-named 280. *Adventurer* (185, JDW 14), dating from 1967, also remained in the Sudan and was scrapped when the contract was over... and Wynns' veteran Tommy Cromwell also retired at the end of the Nyala project, after a lifetime with the company.

Once the project was over, *Conqueror* was one of the trucks disposed of locally... it is doubtful that it has survived!

Transport & Hand
International Enter

In 1982, John Wynn returned from Sudan and told the directors of British Electric Traction (BET), which by this time had taken over United Transport (which, you will remember had purchased Wynns back in the early 1960s) that there was a third big Sudan contract in the offing but it would require an investment of some £75,000 to refurbish and overhaul the tractors and equipment which had already seen such hard service in Sudan.

"Do you have the signed contract?" he was asked. He replied that "things weren't always done that way in the Wynns' world", and was informed that, in that case, there would be no money because "that was how things were done by BET".

THIE also had four Scammell Crusaders tractors with Rolls-Royce Eagle diesel engines. Introduced in 1968, the 6x4 Crusader was popular in Africa and Australia as well as with the British Army.

ing
prise

THIE owned this near-new Scammell Super Constructor with a Rolls-Royce C6SL diesel engine, the last such tractor that Scammell built.

The Super Constructor made a fine sight crossing the desert wastes of Sudan, in this case coupled to ex-Wynns' trailer 456.

Despite never being able to persuade the brakes to operate on more than 16 of the 32 wheels, trailer 456 was used to move two 76-ton condensers across Sudan.

As far as John Wynn was concerned, this was the last straw in what he saw as a sorry saga of big company mis-management and politics, which seemed to involve considerable unnecessary bureaucracy and excessive red tape. Adopting the only course that was available to him, he resigned, an action that ultimately annoyed the Wynns' management so much that they refused to co-operate with him in the months to come even where it would have been in the interests of both parties! At the same time, his cousin Noel elected to take early retirement, almost signalling the end of the involvement of the Wynn family in the business that still bore their name. John's younger son Peter hung on for another two years or so

but, by 1983, the name of 'Wynns' had vanished from the vehicles altogether.

John Wynn's 34-year career with the company which his great grandfather had started had spanned his entire working life. Following his resignation, he believed that he now faced possible unemployment, something which he had never previously contemplated. But, no sooner had word got out that John Wynn was no longer employed by Wynns than Tageldean Elkhazin – known to everyone simply as 'Tag' – proprietor of Enescon got in touch with him and insisted that, with John's help, Enescon could secure the contract to shift two condensers for the British company NEI from the docks at Port Sudan to a new power station which was being constructed in Khartoum – the very contract for which John had been trying, unsuccessfully, to obtain investment from the directors of BET.

Makeshift shower facilities on the road.

John had originally become acquainted with Tag during his previous forays in Sudan. During the course of their conversation, John learned that Tag had already quoted for the job but believed that the magic of the name Wynn would swing it for him. Seemingly with nothing to lose, John agreed and, meeting Tag at a hotel in Newbury, signed an agreement that made him a director of Transport & Handling International Enterprise (THIE), Enescon's local transport company. John's employment with THIE started on 21 June 1982 and ended on 29 May 1983.

It seems that John's involvement was indeed sufficient to ensure that THIE was awarded the NEI contract and John was told that THIE already owned a near-new Scammell Super Constructor with a Rolls-Royce C6SL diesel engine, the last such tractor that

Scammell ever built – as well as a dozen Scammell Crusaders. The Constructor was equipped as a fifth-wheel tractor and had been used for various local heavy haulage jobs. THIE had also purchased two brand-new bonneted Scammell S24 tractors... neither of which, incidentally, it seems was ever paid for! The trucks were painted yellow with white roofs – against the heat of the sun – and proudly displayed the THIE logo on the doors, now including the legend 'with John Wynn', almost as though John were some matinee idol starring in the latest blockbuster!

The company also owned a couple of ex-Wynns' trailers which had been sold to them by BET but, it was clear that if THIE was to undertake any serious heavy haulage work then a hydraulic steering trailer would be required. John had already bought several ex-Wynns' trailers from Peter Sunter following a meeting with Tag and Peter at the Khartoum Hilton on 27 July but, quite by coincidence, Hardwicks at Ewell – now long gone to new housing but, in its day, a yard well-known to all fans of heavy trucks and military-surplus machinery – had ex-Wynns' trailer 456 for sale, an eight-axle double swan-neck unit. The trailer had originally been bought by 'HP' (Percy Wynn) from Cranes back in September 1960, at a cost of £22,500 and, at 22 years of age was, to say the least, well used! It seems that THIE purchased 456 from Hardwicks without John actually knowing which trailer it was before it arrived in Sudan.

Returning to Khartoum on 5 July, John attended his first THIE board meeting five days later, during which there was a power cut... John reports that he was the only one with a torch! A

The first load moved by John Wynn whilst employed by THIE was this large sea-going launch, *Juliet Sarah*, driven around 760 miles from Port Sudan to Khartoum on an ex-Wynns' drop-frame trailer.

John Wynn poses in front of the Super Constructor after conversion to ballast tractor; note the somewhat makeshift concrete and timber ballast.

meeting with the NEI people followed and John took a 2½-hour flight to Port Sudan in an Otter light aircraft. On 11 July he discovered that the first heavy lift for the Khartoum North Power Station project had already been off-loaded on to the quayside. It took a very frustrating ten days to get the first load onto an ex-Wynns low-loader.

In the meantime, the first job undertaken by John during his time

THIE also purchased a pair of brand-new Scammell S24 fifth-wheel tractors – although there is some doubt as to whether they were ever actually paid for. Here, the pair of them are used to move a couple of large transformers.

Standing side-by-side, John and Tageldean (Tag) Elkhazin pose in front of the two Scammell S24s.

THIE's Super Constructor needed some assistance, provided by Wynns' Contractor *Cavalier*, to bring the 76-ton condenser up the Aqabar Pass *en route* to Khartoum Power Station.

with THIE, and one which, in the end, he did almost completely on his own, involved moving a large sea-going launch, *Juliet Sarah*, from Port Sudan to Khartoum, a distance of around 760 miles. The launch was loaded onto one of THIE's ex-Wynns' trailers on 19 July and, coupled to a Scammell Crusader, the outfit took to the road for Khartoum four days later. John felt that he had no option but to take over the controls of the truck from the regular Sudanese driver after only about 20 miles because it had become obvious that the launch would have soon been upside down or worse due to the driver's inexperience with an outsized load. The Crusader's cab was comparatively cramped when compared to the crew cabs of the big Contractors and it was a lonely job but, at least on the outward journey, the launch gave John somewhere a little more spacious to sleep during overnight stops! The launch was safely delivered to Khartoum on 26 July.

By this time the S24 tractors had been shipped to Port Sudan, where the

inevitable paperwork delays at the docks, meant that they sat, unused, on the quayside for several months. Meanwhile, John was becoming increasingly impatient to get started on the NEI project and was delighted when Tag asked him to sort out the situation with the tractors and to bring them to Khartoum North with the two 42-ton transformers. When word finally came from the docks that the trucks could be released John flew back to Port Sudan on 29 July. Before leaving, he asked his new partners where the keys could be found. 'At the dock office' was the reply so, on 7 August 1982, John went down there with a couple of drivers, finding the tractors virtually hidden behind a massive wall of mealie (maize) sacks. Once again, John asked about the keys, and was astonished when one of the drivers took him outside and counted-off so many sacks from one end of the wall, before sticking his hand in between a couple of them – and triumphantly produced the keys! It's difficult to imagine what on earth would have happened had the sacks been shipped

out or had the driver moved on.... but things were done differently there.

It took from 22 July to 9 August to get the two transformers loaded but, finally, the convoy was ready, moving off from Port Sudan on 11 August and arriving, after a lot of tyre problems, at Khartoum on 15 August. And, having, at last, got their hands on the S24s it was galling when one stripped a gear in the main gearbox, necessitating a visit from Colin Betteress, an engineer from Scammell, to sort it out.

John returned to Britain two days later for a few days holiday... and a lot of phone calls. On 13 August he drove up to Stafford to see his son Peter who, at the time, was working for GEC under Mike Williams and was living near Eccleshall. Continuing his journey north John met with the Project Manager for the Khartoum project at NEI in Newcastle-upon-Tyne. He was shown the first of the 76-ton condensers and given drawings that would allow THIE to ensure that the trailers could be prepared to safely accept the load. A useful chat with Glynn Rees at Scammell's Watford factory followed before John drove on to Harpenden on 16 August and thence back to Newport where his car had a puncture just ten miles outside the town. On 22 September, he flew to Zurich, returning to Britain the next day.

By 2 October, John was back in Khartoum and spent a lot of time in having to excuse THIE from using Sudan Rail to bring cargo from Port Sudan, including having to actually off-load an 18-ton transformer which should never have been loaded onto rail cars in the first place. In typical Tag fashion, once he had secured a contract and agreed the price, he would sub-contract elements of it to the railways at a lower price. Having sorted the situation out, NEI were promised that

The last 10 feet of a surplus ex-Wynns' Dyson trailer (328) was cut up to make the ballast body for the Super Constructor. It might not have been pretty but it got the job done.

The Scammell S24 was available in both 6x4 and 6x6 form and shared a cab with the Landtrain. With the right engine, it was capable of some serious hard work and both Mammoet and Econofreight used S24s as tractor units in much the same way that Wynns had used Contractors.

there would be no more rail journeys from Port Sudan.

A week later, John was back in Khartoum before flying to Saudi Arabia en-route to Qatar to assess local transport facilities to move refinery equipment for C A Parsons. Three weeks later he was back in Newport, subsequently returning to Khartoum on 5 November when he accompanied Tag and his wife, flying first class. On 12 November John left for Port Sudan by bus, staying in a very seedy hotel at Kannala before discovering that the bus was so full that the onward journey was impossible and eventually negotiating a taxi ride for which the driver, who seemed reluctant to stay awake for the whole journey, charged £235 (Sudan pounds).

On 15 November, the team started loading vehicles for a run to Sim Sim, for a Canadian Farming Aid organisation. Although it had proved very difficult to get the cargo, consisting of two combine harvesters and several containers of cement loaded, the convoy of trucks, which included four Scammell Crusaders, two S24s and the Contractor artic, eventually left three days later, with John driving a brand-new International tipper, which had just 272km on the clock. One of the S24s was coupled to an ex-Wynns' low-loading trailer, carrying THIE's 25-ton mobile crane, which was going to be required for off-loading at the other end of the journey. Unfortunately, the outfit broke down with hub trouble and

During a run to Sim Sim for a Canadian Farming Aid organisation, THIE used four Scammell Crusaders, two S24s and the Contractor artic, with John Wynn driving a brand-new International tipper.

delayed the convoy for more than a day. There was more trouble when the crews encountered a terrible accident on the Aqabar Pass (with much justification, the word is Arabic for 'difficult'!) just ten miles outside of Port Sudan, where a pick-up truck carrying 14 passengers, both on it and in it, had collided with a DAF artic. The DAF was on the wrong side of the road because it had been overtaking a loaded Fiat that had not moved over into the inside lane. All 14 passengers in the pick-up were killed. John had gone up first to check that the pass was clear whilst the Muslim

convoy drivers were at prayer and it required considerable skill to get all six of the vehicles past the terrible carnage at the scene. Whilst the accident was truly appalling, John was astonished that it never made it into the Sudanese news in Khartoum.

The route, as before, took the trucks by road to Gedareff, some 500 miles from Port Sudan, which took the best part of three days. After this section, the convoy turned off the metalled road, travelling due east for some 100 miles to the site of the farm project. There was no tarmac surface on this section

Scammell Crusader loaded with farm equipment *en route* to Sim Sim... and perhaps not quite operating in the terrain which its makers had envisaged.

at all and the trucks encountered some very soft passages in which the Contractor became bogged down. Two of the Crusaders had to be unloaded to allow them to be used to trans-ship the containers that were on the Contractor. As always in the Sudan, the job took much more time than had been envisaged and John did not get back to Khartoum until 9.45pm on 25 November. The next few days were spent in Khartoum moving equipment from the railhead, including four 70-foot girders that weighed 10 tons and were carried on a 25-foot low loader... This necessitated John showing how birdcage packing could be constructed to support the girders.

At the beginning of December John returned to Britain.

Looking back at the diary which he kept at the time, John recalls how cut-off and isolated he felt working in such a huge country. For example, he had little access to any news medium and it wasn't until 20 November, when he was able to use the radio in the cab of the International tipper that he discovered via the BBC World Service that the Soviet Premier, Leonid Brezhnev, had died ten days earlier.

At the time, the Wynns company was still at work in Sudan moving four 240-ton diesel engines from Port Sudan to Khartoum for a power station project being constructed by Capper Neil. John had negotiated the contract for this project with Capper Neil before resigning from Wynns and had, in his possession, written permission form the Sudanese authorities to transport them on a Nicolas 20-axle flat-top trailer. Hearing that Wynns' John Dixon was flying in to Khartoum Airport on 30 November to supervise the project, on the very same day that John was flying back to Britain, it seemed sensible that the two should meet. Whilst passing on some mail that he had brought with him for John, Dixon was much amused when he realised that John was, up to that moment, unaware that the trailer which THIE had purchased from Hardwicks was the old number 456. Nevertheless, he readily agreed, against company orders but in a spirit of friendship and loyalty to John, that he would supervise the offloading of this trailer from the RoRo ship and get it to THIE's yard at Port Sudan.

John arrived back in Britain on 2 December, subsequently making visits to Harpenden and London as well as making a lot of phone calls to Sudan. He was back in Khartoum by 20 December and left two days later for Port Sudan, scarcely enjoying the 12-hour, 750-mile trip at an average speed of 60mph... in a Toyota pick-up truck in which he had to carry his own fuel for the entire journey!

It had become apparent to John by this time that the fifth-wheel configuration of the Super Constructor meant that, unless something was done, it was going to spend its life unable to do anything but haul semi-trailers, which seriously restricted its usefulness to the company. John struggled to convince the THIE staff of the importance of being able to use the tractor with draw-bar trailers but, eventually, the decision was taken to build a ballast body to fit across the chassis over the fifth-wheel, which would make the tractor more versatile. The notion of placing ballast over the rear wheels to increase traction was totally new to the Sudanese crews but a body was constructed locally by effectively cannibalising the last ten feet of ex-Wynns' trailer 328, a Dyson unit which, by that time, everyone had agreed was redundant. When completed, the tractor was able to tow ex-Wynns' trailer 456, which was a 32-wheel unit, and this gave the best of both worlds. The tractor could now be readily converted from one configuration to the other, increasing its versatility.

The ship carrying the first of the 76-ton condensers docked on Christmas Day 1982 but, since it was being carried in the bottom of the hold, it was obvious that the condenser would not be available to the THIE crews until early January. In fact, it wasn't unloaded from the ship until 7 January, by which time the Super Constructor had been fitted with its ballast body. A dozen huge concrete blocks were loaded into the ballast box and the fuel tank was strapped on top of them, bringing the total weight of the truck up to about 21 tons. However, one other problem was that THIE still lacked someone who was experienced with hydraulic trailers. John thought he knew just the man, Colin Kilby, who had worked with Wynns as a steersman for years, was out of work and John managed to persuade him to join THIE in the Sudan. Everything was now in place to move two 76-ton condensers. At the docks, the first condenser was loaded onto trailer 456 and the crew ran the outfit around the dock roads to check the steering and brakes – they were not impressed! It was a 32-wheeled trailer, but John recalls that they never could persuade the brakes

Two more of the four Crusaders on the road – such as it is – to Sim Sim, loaded with farm aid.

Even the best-laid road surfaces in parts of the Sudan were not quite what they seemed and the convoy was frequently delayed by having to dig the trucks out of trouble.

on more than 16 of the wheels to operate. Nevertheless, this was the trailer on which they moved the two 76-ton condensers across Sudan so clearly the Sudanese authorities took a fairly relaxed view of such matters!

Whilst the Rolls-Royce engined Super Constructor was plenty powerful, John took the view that two tractors would be required to get the load up the Aqabar Pass. He elected to approach Wynns who, at the time, were still working in Sudan on the Capper Neil project.

Peter Sunter, who had taken over the management of the Capper Neil job when John had quit, had persuaded the Sudanese that three more tractors were required on the project, together with what John describes as 'more wheels'... meaning extra bogies. Permission had already been obtained to use a 20-line flat top trailer but Sunter, anxious to make his own mark and perhaps increase the profitability of the job, changed the specification of the job to use four sets of seven wheels. All of this equipment, including the tractors, was still in the country and, believing that a Wynns' Contractor would be just the job to provide the additional power that he needed, John Wynn asked John Dixon for assistance. It seems that Dixon had been instructed not to assist John without prior approval from Britain and, although this approval was eventually granted, it came at a price

and Wynns agreed to provide one of their Contractors, for half a day... at a (1983) price of £900, rather than the £150-200 that might have been charged in Britain!

They say that 'what goes around comes around' and this meanness of spirit had its consequences. John had little choice about involving Wynns since he knew that he would not have been able to hold the Super

Constructor with the load on the Aqabar Pass. However, once word got back to Britain about how Wynns had treated John, and the consequent risks to the project, NEI was sufficiently upset to refuse to give Wynns, the company, any more work.

But meanwhile, Wynns had completed the Capper Neil project on 27 January 1983, meaning that the Wynns' Contractor was available to

The Coles crane proved invaluable when it was necessary to reduce the weight on the trailers in order to extricate the trucks.

Locals watch the convoy pass, the Crusaders loaded with equipment bound for Sim Sim.

assist in the move to the power station site at Khartoum and, the next day, with the first condenser loaded, the outfit moved off from the lay-by where John had left it a week earlier. With Len Dobie at the wheel of Wynns' Contractor *Cavalier* (Wynns' fleet number 628, XAX 512T) the two big Scammells rolled out of Port Sudan ready for the climb up the Aqabar Pass. When the convoy reached the pass, a policeman was despatched to the top of the climb to hold back on-coming traffic. Lacking any sort of radio equipment, the only way that he could communicate with the convoy was to ask the last vehicle going down to tell the convoy that it could start its ascent!

The climb started and, using only second and third gears, the impressive convoy began the long ascent, reaching the top an hour later at 14.00 hours. Here, the team paused for a well-deserved break and, with its work completed, the Wynns' Contractor returned to Port Sudan. The journey resumed at 06.00 hours the next morning and, for the rest of the 750-mile run, the Super Constructor took the load on its own, stopping every two hours for 15 minutes and finishing at 17.00 hours each evening. There were problems with the hydraulics on the trailer, which slowed the convoy down,

but the load arrived at the Khartoum Power Station site at 10.15 on 4 February, eight days after setting out. The condenser was unloaded two days before the trailer was reduced in width for the journey back to Port Sudan, leaving on 8 February.

During the return journey, the tractor developed a bad air leak in the gearbox which made it impossible to change down and, after just 45 miles, John was forced to park-up and request that a fitter be sent to repair it. The journey resumed at 11.00 hours on 10 February but the air leak was still causing problems and, the next day, a Wynns' pick-up driven by John Dixon came to the stranded truck and invited the crew to come with them some ten miles or so to where they were parked with the second Capper Neil engine. After a nice chat and a cup of tea, it was agreed that young Tom Cromwell – the son of the older Tommy Cromwell – would come back to the Super Constructor and take a look at the gearbox. Strictly against the instructions of the Wynns' management, who had told the men that they were not to provide any assistance to John or THIE, Cromwell sorted out the problem and John was able to resume his journey, pulling into Port Sudan at 12.30 hours on 13 February.

Flying back to Britain via Khartoum, John took a few days off before driving to Newcastle for another meeting with the NEI people. Once again, the journey back to Newport entailed stop-offs at Harpenden and Watford. Following visits to Copenhagen, Redditch, Barking and Rotterdam John returned to Sudan on 1 April and there were several acrimonious meetings with Gordon Daniel of Wynns regarding the high rental charges for the Contractor. John resolved that he would move the second condenser without assistance from Wynns.

The second move was started on 20 April and was accomplished with one of the S24 tractors coupled to a Systems trailer on which some 25 tons of cargo were positioned as far as forward as possible in an effort to ballast the rear wheels. Together with the Super Constructor, this provided the power required. The local man who was driving the S24 was told to stay in first gear up the pass, as did John, driving the Super Constructor. It worked and they completed the climb... but, with the benefit of hindsight, John believes that the gear ratios of the two trucks were so badly mismatched that it might have been better if the S24 had used second gear. During the long climb up the pass, he became very conscious of the lack of big company back-up, and started to wonder whether he had done the right thing in leaving Wynns.

The second condenser arrived in Khartoum at 12.30 hours on 26 April and was unloaded the next day. John took some more days off and then returned to Khartoum on 17 May where he worked for another week. After a long chat with Tag, who thanked him effusively for what he had accomplished, it was obvious that the two men were going to go their separate ways and, on 29 May, John Wynn's employment with THIE was terminated and he returned to Britain wondering what fate had in store.

But things have a way of working out for the best... and other projects were in the offing, in other corners of the globe. •

Well-loaded, the Super Constructor leads the convoy through the scrub.

Flashback...

Hydrocon (derived from the name *Hydraulic Construction*) Highlander
5-ton hydraulic crane unit, new in October 1964.

Guy Warrior tractor
coupled to a tank
trailer. Wynns was the
main South Wales
dealer for Guy Motors
from the end of 1959,
and over a period of
five or more years, the
fleet included a number
of Invincible, Warrior
and Big J trucks.

New Scammell draw-bar tractor dating from the early 1950s.

Scammell Crusader 6x4 tractor unit. This is one of the so-called 100-ton Crusaders – sometimes described as Amazon or CR100 – that appeared at the 1977 Commercial Motor Show in Wynns' livery.

Acquired in 1968, this Scammell Trunker 2 tractor is coupled to a stainless-steel tank trailer.

The other side of the

With the last Sudan project behind him, John returned to Britain in 1983, where he took on a spell of agency driving with Newport transport contractors Overdrive, as well as with Richard Thomas, a former Wynns' transport manager who was now managing the transport for a magazine distributor employing 40ft curtain-side artics.

It was unexciting work for a man used to the responsibility of devising the ways and means of shifting overweight and oversized loads and, as the year drew to a close, John found that he was possibly facing the prospect of unemployment again. However, in November, he received a call from an old friend. Glynn Rees, of Scammell, had known John a long time and wanted to know if he could recommend an ex-Wynns driver for

The S24 that was assigned to John Wynn was the most powerful truck on site and, initially, was used for moving plant... typical loads included this aggregate crusher.

Aerial view of the *Merchant Providence* showing the permanent moorings and the rise-and-fall roadway. With no proper dockside facilities available, this was the only way of unloading equipment on the island.

Scammell S24 negotiating a load off the *Merchant Providence* that was used as a permanent floating jetty-head at East Cove, with a rise-and-fall roadway of Bailey bridge sections actually welded to it.

THE GOVERNMENT OF THE FALKLAND ISLANDS

£1

A031694

THESE NOTES ARE LEGAL TENDER FOR THE PAYMENT OF ANY AMOUNT

ONE POUND

1ST OCTOBER 1984

FOR THE GOVERNMENT OF THE FALKLAND ISLANDS

THE GOVERNMENT OF THE FALKLAND ISLANDS

world

Three empty low-loader trailers coupled to the S24.

an S24 tractor which Scammell had just sold to a joint-venture consortium of Laing, Mowlem and Amey Roadstone (LMA) which was constructing a new military airfield on the Falkland Islands. Not knowing that he was out of work, Glynn was surprised when John said that he would be prepared to take on the job. However, Glynn was well aware that John was more than capable and said that he would call Roger Venthen of LMA and give him John's number.

As a result of this, John found himself travelling to Surbiton, Surrey where LMA had their headquarters. The formal interview was followed by a medical examination in which John was asked if he still had his appendix. "No," he said, "it was removed when I was 18". Apparently, it was company policy that all workers had an appendectomy before sailing, since the lack of suitable medical facilities on the

Islands could have presented a potentially fatal situation had any of the workers developed appendicitis during their time in the South Atlantic. With all of the necessary formalities completed, John was flown from Heathrow to Cape Town on 5 December 1983, where he boarded the MV *England* at 5.00pm the same day, bound for the distant Falkland Islands.

John was employed as a 'heavy plant operator' on a fixed salary for a 14-month tour of duty, which included one spell back in Britain. He was scheduled to complete his contract in January 1985 which meant that he would spend two Christmases away from home. In recognition of weather conditions on the Falklands he was issued with two heavy-duty long-sleeved pullovers, two pairs of woollen socks, one pair of work boots, one balaclava, two pairs of gloves, one pair of safety Wellingtons, and a snorkel jacket.

The Falkland Islands remains the most distant outpost of the once great British Empire. Located in the South Atlantic Ocean, some 300 miles from the coast of mainland South America, the Falklands archipelago consists of two main islands, East Falkland and West Falkland, as well as 776 smaller islands. Stanley, on East Falkland, is the capital and the Islands are a self-governing Overseas Territory of the United Kingdom. The climate is not hospitable and the on-shore wind frequently howls across the treeless landscape with the temperature rarely climbing above 77°F, even at the height of summer, and often measured in single figures. Now, look at a map and see how far the Falklands Islands are from the nearest land, which is either South Africa or South America... This is a stretch of water so desolate that John says he saw just four other ships during his two return trips to the Islands!

Ever since the re-establishment of British rule on the Islands in 1833, Argentina had claimed sovereignty of

Caterpillar D902 heavy 'dozer loaded onto a low-loading plant trailer with a detachable swan neck; the weight of the 'dozer is just under 50 tons.

With a capacity of around 40 tons, the NCK Andes C41B excavator was widely used in extracting stone from the local quarries.

what they called Islas Malvinas. In pursuit of this claim, which continues to be rejected by the Islanders, Argentina invaded in 1982, precipitating the two-month-long undeclared Falklands War. The eventual result, at some cost in lives on both sides, was the defeat and withdrawal of the Argentine forces. The Falklands War was, perhaps, Margaret Thatcher's greatest triumph but, after the euphoria of the surrender of Argentine forces and the retaking of the

Islands in June 1982, the British Government believed that the Falkland Islands remained vulnerable to air attack from Argentina and wanted to keep aircraft available if necessary. The existing airfield at Port Stanley had been repaired following an RAF interdiction raid that had placed a 500 lb bomb on the centre of the runway, denying it to Argentine forces, but, even so, it was unsuitable for use by jet aircraft. The Royal Navy kept an

King low-loader trailer with four brand-new Caterpillar L406 loaders.

Aggregate conveyor equipment carried on a skeleton trailer.

aircraft carrier moored off the coast, protecting the Islands against possible raids with its Sea Harriers. HMS *Hermes* was the first such vessel, replaced by HMS *Invincible*, before the role was passed to the newly-constructed HMS *Illustrious*.

Clearly this situation could not continue and, deciding that the existing Stanley airfield was never going to be suitable for a permanent base, the Government determined to construct a new RAF station and military base on the Islands. One option was to enlarge or extend the Port Stanley facility; the other possibility identified a new site for an airfield at Mount Pleasant. In August 1982, Property Services Agency (PSA) teams began preliminary surveys of the two possible sites. A full-time PSA team was assigned to the project in February 1983 and, a month later, tenders were invited from seven

interested contractors, six of them forming three consortia to better manage the work. On 27 June, the British Parliament announced that the Mount Pleasant site posed fewer construction difficulties and had been selected as the lower-cost option. At the same time, a contract was awarded to LMA, a joint-venture consortium established by Laing, Mowlem and Amey Roadstone. At £190 million, the contract represented an eye-watering 4 per cent of that year's total British defence budget!

The project covered the design and construction of a new airport, complete with supporting accommodation and services. At its height, this massive undertaking would employ more than 2,000 men for the best part of two years. Completion was scheduled for early 1986, but the temporary road between Mount Pleasant and Port

Stanley was to be handed over in April 1985. Separate contracts were also issued to LMA for the road linking the site to Port Stanley, and for the Ministry of Defence (MoD) communications equipment and navigational aids, bringing the total cost to £215 million.

The construction work included building a main runway, 8,500 feet long, together with a 5,000ft-long secondary runway, the two runways being arranged in an 'X' shape so that one was always correctly oriented to the prevailing winds. There were also hard-standings for passenger and military aircraft and helicopters, a hangar for wide-bodied jets, and an air-traffic control tower. In addition, the base would have water-supply facilities, and a 7.5MW power station with 3MW standby generators. The work also covered all of the ancillary buildings and accommodation required for up to 2,000 personnel who would be stationed on, and operate, the base. A half-mile long corridor would link the barracks, mess facilities and recreational and welfare areas of the base, leading to the locals giving it the nickname 'Death Star', a fictional moon-sized space ship and planet-destroying super weapon appearing in the *Star Wars* movies, because of the often, confusing layout of the buildings.

One of the real challenges of the project was distance, because almost everything required, including personnel, plant and vehicles, materials and construction equipment, had to be shipped to the Islands from Britain. The only exception was that the stone and aggregate required would be sourced from the Islands and the original PSA

John poses by a Caterpillar D903 'dozer, loaded onto one of the King trailers.

70-ton rock-crushing equipment bound for the quarries. By the end of the project, almost 2 million cubic yards of rock had been excavated, and more than 1.5 million tons of stone crushed.a

survey team had already identified potential quarry sites. By the time the project was completed, almost 2 million cubic yards of rock had been excavated, and more than 1.5 million tons of stone had been crushed by LMA, working around the clock.

The second problem was one of communications. There was no effective link between the airport site and Britain, and thus the outside world, except via an undersea cable at Port Stanley some 30 miles distant. The British company Cable & Wireless eventually established an earth station at Port Stanley, linked to the site offices at Mount Pleasant, to provide satellite communications to Britain.

In September 1983, the MV *Merchant Providence*, purchased by LMA especially for the project, set sail on the 8,000-mile voyage from Britain, with the pioneer workforce on board, as well as 13,600 tons of cargo and equipment. A month later, *Merchant Providence* berthed at East Cove located on the southern-most edge of East Falkland. Meanwhile, a second ship, *England*, chartered from Cunard, had set sail from Tilbury at the end of September, carrying a further 76 construction workers. All of the workers who followed travelled, firstly, by air to Johannesburg or Cape Town from Heathrow, with the near 12-hour flight being followed by a ten- or 11-day boat

trip across the South Atlantic. The alternative, which would have entailed flying to Argentina and then taking a boat to the Falklands, was politically out of the question because of Argentina's continued claim on the Islands. The *England* continued to work a monthly schedule between Cape Town and East Cove and, as the contract progressed, four chartered cargo vessels also sailed in turn from Avonmouth about every three weeks and, by April 1985, there had been about 22 sailings carrying something like 513,000 tons of materials, plant and equipment.

There were no suitable port facilities on the Islands, which could have

One of three Steelfield cement-batching plants, each weighing 45 tons. The first was fitted with tandem-wheel running gear that allowed it to be coupled directly to the tractor and towed. The plan to remove this running gear and attach it to the second and third loads was eventually abandoned.

Using a Caterpillar excavator to help place a load on a flat-top trailer.

created difficulties in moving all of the equipment ashore. This problem was solved by using the *Merchant Providence* as a permanent floating jetty-head at East Cove, with a rise-and-fall roadway, comprising sections of Bailey bridge, actually welded to it. Every incoming ship moored alongside the jetty-head and unloaded onto the deck of the *Merchant Providence*, with trucks then used to move the supplies ashore.

A temporary construction village was established close to the unloading facility, and work started on a temporary six-mile access road to the airport site. The road was completed a month later. On 31 December 1983 there was a turf-cutting ceremony on the main runway by the Commander of British Forces and, by April, the workforce had moved to a more permanent location on the site. The temporary accommodation facility at East Cove was dismantled.

John's first few days on the Islands were naturally a bit chaotic but he quickly settled down into the routine of 12-hour working days, six or seven days a week. When the site transport manager discovered the background of this mysterious John Wynn, he was actually offered the job of managing all of the transport resources on site, a role

that he rejected... although he was the senior driver on the project. As a driver, John was assigned to one of a fleet of six tractors that had been purchased by the LMA consortium and shipped to the Islands on the *Merchant Providence*. There were seven Leyland T43 6x4 Landtrains, and a single Scammell S24 6x4 fifth-wheel tractor, assigned fleet number L3, which John knew would become 'his' tractor. Having spent months in the Sudan desert peering across the long bonnet of a Super Constructor, John felt right at home in the cab of the big S24 as he surveyed the barren Falkland Islands' landscape, even if the outside temperature was not quite what he was used to. Thank the Lord for those woolly jumpers and snorkel jackets!

Introduced in 1980, the Scammell S24 was the last heavy tractor to be developed before Scammell was wound-up by Leyland in 1988. Constructed in both 6x4 and 6x6 configurations, and more rarely as a 4x2, the S24 was effectively an uprated version of the export-only Leyland T43 Landtrain. It was offered as either a standard heavy-duty truck chassis on which the customer could mount the body of his choice, or as a prime mover for operation at a gross train weight of up to 300 tons. The standard power

unit was the 14-litre Cummins NTE350, at first in combination with a Spicer gearbox and Brockhouse torque converter, but later machines were equipped with an Allison automatic transmission. The truck was too wide for normal road use in Britain but was eminently suitable for 'STGO CAT 3' work where the normal rules regarding weights, axle loadings and dimensions don't apply, and was popular with British heavy-haulage operators during the 1980s and into the 1990s. It was even offered as a tank transporter.

Of course, the size and weight of the trucks was of little consequence on the Falkland Islands since they were never used on the road.

Of the seven Landtrains, five were equipped with fifth wheels for use with semi-trailers, whilst two more were fitted with huge dump bodies to assist in Tarmacadam surfacing and concrete-pavement laying. However, John's S24 was the most powerful of the trucks and, initially, was used for moving plant around the site – typical loads included a 70-ton aggregate crusher, a clutch of Caterpillar D9 'dozers, and a big NCK-Rapier C60 crane. However, the fifth wheel on the S24 had been sized to suit a particular King low-loader trailer which meant that John was unable to couple to any of the 40-foot trailers and semi-trailers which were available on site. Scammell's Glynn Rees, in far-off Watford, came to the rescue by providing an adaptor which would allow the truck to be coupled to other trailers and, in the meantime, John drove Landtrain number L7.

Interestingly, at least one of the Falklands' tractors later returned to Britain where it survived into the 1990s, re-registered, modified and operated by George Curtis of South Humberside as an 8x4 ballast tractor, the extra axle being necessary to meet, then, new British axle-loading regulations. It is also worth noting that the S24 was one of the three Scammell trucks that, at least in theory, was also available from Unipower when that organisation took over some of Scammell's operation in 1988, the others being the military Commander and the Nubian.

Once the fifth-wheel adaptor arrived, the S24 could be used with any of the mixed bag of LMA trailers and one of its first jobs was to move an NCK-Rapier Ajax 680 excavator on a King 75-ton low-loader trailer. John was also pleased to discover that the job was far from straightforward, often calling for a degree of ingenuity. However, the weather on the Falkland Islands was a permanent obstacle to the work, often with sun, rain, snow, hail and gale force winds experienced within the space of a single day and there were many days

Some loads were easier to handle than others; this conveyor equipment has its own wheels to simplify movement.

when the wind was blowing the rain horizontally across the treeless landscape and John was huddled down by the tractor trying to tighten something up, when he wondered why he had taken on the job at all.

On Christmas Day 1983 John was asked to 'prove' that the access Bailey-bridge section, which had been welded to the deck of the *Merchant Providence*, would allow the trucks to either reverse onto the deck, or to drive on forwards and turn round on the deck itself. This was obviously crucial to the success of the unloading operation. With a crowd of 'suits' watching, John brought one of the Leyland T43 Landtrains, complete with a 40-foot trailer, onto the deck and successfully turned it around, earning a bottle of Scotch for his boss, Larry Larsen.

In the New Year, things settled down into a regular routine as the S24 was used to move a variety of items, ranging from containers – some of which were loaded with explosives for use in the quarries – to prefabricated housing packs, 60-ton stone crushers, Caterpillar D5, D8 and D9 bulldozers, fork-lift trucks, dump trucks, etc, etc.

The loads that caused the biggest headache were three Steelfield cement-batching plants, each weighing 45 tons and measuring 30 feet in length, more than ten feet in width, and with a height of 13 feet. The first one to arrive came complete with tandem-wheel running gear that allowed it to be coupled directly to the tractor and towed, although it was not easy to shunt it around on the deck of the *Providence* to get lined-up to take the load down the ramp. The original plan had been to remove the running gear from the first of the plants and to attach it to the second and third when they arrived from Britain. It was a time-consuming

Careful packing was required to secure this conveyor equipment.

process and, perhaps not surprisingly, Larry Larsen asked if it would be possible to load the batching plant onto a semi-trailer straight off the deck of the *Merchant Providence*. However, whilst John agreed that it was, in theory, possible, in practice the Bailey-bridge section of the ramp was too narrow to allow the low-loader to be reversed up onto the deck and, to make matters worse, the load was top heavy and had a high centre of gravity.

The second plant was loaded on 27 January 1984 but it took over an hour to tie it down sufficiently securely for John to be confident that he could negotiate the ramp. This led to a heated argument between John and the foreman in charge of off-loading the ship since the operation was blocking the ramp and delaying everything else. Politely, John pointed out that the batching plant had come 8,000 miles from Britain and that it wouldn't be too clever to tip it off the trailer when the tractor negotiated the bad camber as it turned left off the ramp. Having seen how much the load heeled over on the

turn, the foreman did at least have the good grace to seek John out later that night and apologise for having tried to rush him.

Finally, once the two loads were safely off the ship and transferred to the lay-down area, it was relatively easy to get them onto the low-loader and run them up to the location where they were to be used.

In addition to these three units, there were three 60-foot conveyors for the aggregate crusher which presented a problem as they tended to whip if not properly supported. The conveyors were moved on a 40-foot three-axle trailer, but needed special birdcage packing constructed to support each one in an upright position during the move.

John's first tour of duty on the Islands ended on 11 June and he returned home on the *England*, arriving two weeks later. By 24 July, he was back at Heathrow for the flight to Cape Town, setting foot on the Falklands again on 7 August after a long sea voyage but, returning to the Islands, John discovered that everything had changed in his two-month absence. The trucks were now being worked 24 hours a day in an attempt to meet the schedule, and his new working day started at 19.00 hours and finished at 07.00. Sometimes John was driving truck number L3, sometimes a six-wheel T43 Landtrain tipper, sometimes a forklift truck, and occasionally a big Terex shovel loading aggregate at one of the three quarries on the Islands. Trailers were regularly abused and overloaded and, equally, a typical week could also involve moving 7-8,000 tons of cement or bitumen up to the airport site, either from a ship or from the lay-down area. And, since all of the heavy equipment had been moved to its working location, the King low-loader trailer was virtually surplus to requirements, which was probably just as well since it was scarcely in the first flush of youth. When unloading

This batching plant couples directly to the fifth wheel of the tractor and can be towed on its own wheels.

Caterpillar D8 'dozers over the side, John had always packed the chassis to prevent it from being twisted. During his absence, others had been less careful and the constant pressure to rush the unloading had led to the swan neck and the locating pins of the trailer being cracked.

So, all things considered, John's second period on the Islands was a complete contrast to the first, whilst being no less interesting.

Astonishingly, the contract was completed according to the schedule and the airfield was opened in 1985 by Prince Andrew who, of course, was a veteran of the Falklands' campaign. It was fully completed the following year and, on 15 January 1985, John started the return journey to Britain aboard the MV *England*, arriving in Cape Town on 28 January ready for the long flight back to Heathrow the following day.

His enduring memories of the Falkland Islands included stunning sunrises and sunsets, the relentless winds that howled across the treeless landscape for much of the time, and the feeling of having been part of a worthwhile project. On the downside, it was strange that none of the Islanders thought to supply the contractors' canteen with any of the fresh fish that was in abundance all around – 90 per cent of the food came from refrigerated containers.

Loaded with the NCK Andes C41B excavator, John allows a Volvo-BM articulated loader to pass by.

New ventures, new lands

John stands in front of a trailer loaded with an Omani Army Qayis Al Ardh tank, based on the British Chieftain.

Once the Falkland Islands contract was complete, John returned to Britain with little idea of what he was going to do next. As it happens, he wasn't unemployed for long and, in February 1985, within a month or so of returning, found himself on the other side of the world, in Hong Kong, and back behind the wheel of a big Scammell. This time, he was working on a power station contract.

John had been called at his home in February 1985, and asked if he could attend a meeting at GEC's plant in Stafford to discuss moving a large amount of power-station equipment, which included a number of 125-135-ton transformers, as well as associated switchgear and generators. The equipment had been manufactured by GEC English Electric at Stafford and was to be shipped to Hong Kong by sea where it was to be off-loaded at the docks and moved to a lay-down area. From here, the equipment was to be called-off for delivery to various sites across the islands, including one at Castle Peak, where the China Light & Power Company (CLP) was building electricity-generating stations. CLP owned three Cummins-engined 100-ton Scammell Contractors, together with a bonneted S24 and a 48-wheel trailer, which they were using to shift the heavy electrical equipment. All of the equipment was pre-owned, having come from Wrekin Roadways in Britain.

Founded in 1901, China Light & Power was one of a number of electricity suppliers in Hong Kong. The company had started in a small way and, in the first year of operation, the maximum demand for power was just 1,000kW, but CLP had built its first power station in 1903 and, by 1969, had opened its largest plant, a 1,520MW oil-fired station at Tsing Yi as part of an ambitious programme of expansion and fuel diversification to bring electricity to all parts of the Territory. In 1984, CLP had taken over the Cheung Chau Power Company and had started work on the 1,400MW Castle Peak coal-fired power station, which opened in 1986.

John was not in at the beginning of the project, although one other ex-Wynns' man, Ron Savage, had been involved from the beginning. Ron and John flew to Hong Kong together on 27 February 1985, and had supervised the move of the first 125-ton transformer to Castle Peak, a move which it would be fair to say had not gone well. Despite coupling all three tractors together, the Cummins-powered Contractors had been unable to pull the combined 300-ton train weight up a 1:4 section of Hammer Hill at Wong Tai Sin. Stalled on the incline, but with reversing out of

Military engineers' plant loaded and ready to roll.

Mack and Mercedes-Benz tractors were the weapons of choice on the Hamdan Oman contract.

Although designed for highway use, this Mercedes-Benz 6x4 tractor proved itself to be very capable.

A pair of 6x4 Macks coupled to LPG tankers.

the question, the convoy came to a halt. The crew chocked as many wheels as they could but it was essential to keep the engines running to maintain brake pressure and, for 90 minutes the convoy sat there while the crew waited nervously for assistance from the British Army. Eventually, a Scammell Commander tank-transporter tractor turned up and coupled its huge 20-ton Rotzler winch to the lead tractor. With the additional pull of the Commander's winch, and the combined tractive effort of the three Contractors which were coupled to the trailer, the load was finally brought up the hill, before being delivered to Castle Peak.

John had arrived in Hong Kong before the second load set off and, keen not to repeat the difficulties encountered with the first transformer, John and Ron Savage got hold of a powerful four-wheel drive Michigan wheeled loading shovel. Filling the shovel with as much aggregate as they could (in order to provide ballast), the loader was coupled to the Contractors to provide additional power on the uphill section. It was an unconventional, some might say bold, move but with two of the tractors and the shovel at the front, and the third tractor pushing, it still took the best part of three hours to get the load up the hill. During the entire duration of the climb John had to clamp both hands onto his right knee, holding his foot onto the throttle to ensure that the tractor was running at full revs. Later, John said that this was the steepest hill he had ever encountered during his years in heavy haulage and that the climb was a nail-biting experience from start to finish... but there was no doubt that the additional power had done the trick.

With this part of the project out of the way, the British team was free to concentrate on training the Chinese

In direct contrast to what had been going on in Oman and Hong Kong, John also spent a period driving for a Newport agency, often finding himself behind the wheel of nothing more exciting than this Leyland 6x4 tractor.

The Hong Kong crew. From left to right, John Wynn, Colin Kilby, Ray Purnell, Ron Savage and Roger Harris.

The China Light & Power Company (CLP) owned three Cummins-engined 100-ton Scammell Contractors, together with a bonneted S24 and a 48-wheel trailer, which they were using to shift the heavy electrical equipment. All of the equipment had come from Wrekin Roadways.

crews who were to take over for the future.

On 29 April 1985, with his role in Hong Kong effectively over, John returned to Britain and eventually found himself based back at Newport after replying to an advertisement in the local paper for HGV drivers for British Steel at the former Lysaghts' plant – where his grandfather had put in the original 40-ton bed plates back in 1890. He spent the eight months from

May to December driving a Leyland Marathon delivering steel to a host of customers in South and Southwest Wales, and then uncoupling the empty trailers at the steel plant in Margam and bringing up loaded trailers of steel to Laysaghts or Llanwern.

But by the new year, John was off to foreign parts again when Tageldean 'Tag' Elkhazin popped up again.

'Tag' was proprietor of Ensecon and an old friend of John. The two men had

already worked together in Sudan but now Tag was also running a recruitment agency for top-flight transport personnel. 'Tag' telephoned in December 1983, just two days after John had returned from the Falkland Islands, and wanted to know if John was interested in a job in Oman where the Hamdan Trading Group, based in the Sultanate of Oman, was bidding for a US Army contract to move military materiel. It seems that the man that had originally been employed by 'Tag' was not up to the mark and he was seeking a replacement.

John's foreman at Lysaghts, Keith Davies, agreed to let John go and also suggested that he was pretty sure that there would still be a job available when he returned from Oman. On the morning of 5 January 1986, John took down the Christmas decorations at home with his then wife, Mo, and in the evening flew from Heathrow to Muscat. Uncertain as to exactly what was expected of him when he arrived in Oman, John spent much of the seven-hour flight making out a list of questions, the answers to which he hoped would clarify his role.

Arriving in Oman, John met some of the Hamdan people at Muscat Airport and was shown his accommodation which consisted of a bungalow in the Hamdan yard! The set-up seemed more than satisfactory, even if the accommodation was a little basic, and John learned that he would be in

Riding shotgun in the ballast box of one of the Contractors... and adding little to the ballast!

John watches the as the CLP driver manoeuvres the transformer loaded onto the 48-wheel trailer.

charge in Muscat with the title of General Manager (North) and would have the use of a Toyota Crown... once he'd passed an Oman driving test! Dick Simmons was based at Hamdan's headquarters, an hour away by air at Salalah.

The next day John went with Dick to the offices of the US Army Detachment 3, 4448 MOBSS ('Mobilization Support System') where they met with Colonel Chuck Jurgensen who explained what was wanted and gave John some useful pointers. Hamdan's quotation was delivered to the US Army on 18 January and there were further meetings with Jurgensen at the Novotel. Four companies were competing for the

work but it seemed that Jurgensen was keen that Hamdan get the contract, perhaps because Hamdan was the only company with the benefit of the experience of John Wynn, and John was the first white manager of the company who could drive all of the trucks – including reversing them – as well as being able to rope and sheet loads better than most of the 100 or so mostly Indian drivers. Naturally, the contract went to Hamdan.

The materiel was shipped from the USA to Salalah and then trucked to a US base adjacent to Seeb Airport, near Muscat. Separately, ammunition was brought directly off the coast of Oman by US Navy ships before being moved

by tug and barge to Jasirat Masirah Island, off the east coast of the Sultanate, 225 miles and some 30 minutes flying time from Muscat.

A former RAF airfield that had been returned to the Royal Air Force of Oman, Masirah remained a closed military area and in 1975, Oman had offered the use of the island base to the USA. In 1980, the two Governments had concluded a ten-year 'facilities access' agreement which granted the US forces limited access to the air base on Masirah, plus other bases at Thamarit and As Sib, and to naval bases at Muscat, Salalah, and Al Khasab. After the Iranian Revolution in 1979, the US Government had spent a

All of the CLP trucks and trailers, including the three Scammell Contractors, were formerly owned by Wrekin Roadways in Britain.

John Wynn and the CLP transport crew.

lot of money on airfields in friendly Middle Eastern countries and since 1981 there has been an ongoing programme to 'harden' and upgrade Oman's key airfields, including the construction of hardened aircraft shelters (HAS), the lengthening and strengthening of runways, and the development of extensive support facilities, ordnance depots and fuel dumps. Masirah was being used as a massive arsenal where the US Army was apparently stockpiling materiel against the very real possibility of serious conflict in the region. This later proved to be a wise move because the Masirah arsenal was able to assist with Operation Desert Shield, the build-up to the First Gulf War in 1990.

Hamdan's transport resources included bonneted and forward-control Mercedes-Benz tractors, some heavy-

John Wynn and Scammell's Glynn Rees in Oman.

duty bonneted Macks, a rough-terrain crane, and a selection of flat-bed and tank-transporter trailers. However, this wasn't the whole story because the last part of the journey meant that the materiel had to be moved to the island by flat-bottom barge. Perhaps not a natural sailor it was during one of the sea-going parts of the operation that John had an accident that resulted in him waking up in the base hospital at Masirah, with a US plane waiting to possibly evacuate him to Muscat for treatment. Happily this proved unnecessary but John was not shy about taking advantage of other US Army facilities, and enjoyed 'rest and recreation' at the base during his off-duty hours.

As had been the case in Hong Kong, part of Hamdan's role was to train the local labour, and this included showing Omani military personnel how to multiply the pull on a winch by using snatch blocks.

John was in Oman from 6 January 1986 to 15 December 1987. It was a long time to be away from home so he was delighted when his then wife, Mo, was able to join him for a month, which included his birthday, in October 1986. Without doubt, the contract was a real life-saver for John who had always found that once you have proved that you know what you are doing to Americans, and have shown that you are prepared to work hard, they are great people to deal with. At the end of the contract he was presented with a plaque which read *'John Wynn. Sincere appreciation for dedicated support, 16 October 1986'*. It remains one of his proudest mementoes.

When the Oman contract came to an end, John returned to Britain. By

this time, he was 56 and had no particular desire to continue globe-trotting. He needed something more permanent and resumed his job as an HGV1 driver at British Steel on 8 March 1988. During this spell at British Steel, John drove three different tractors, numbers 3, 6 and 18, covering a total of 120,000 miles back and forth from Llanwern to Margam, West Wales, the Midlands and London, with the trailers loaded with steel.

And then came the incident that changed his life.

One fateful day in 1994, having made a Midlands delivery the previous day, John was running the tractor empty back to Llanwern form Lysaghts preparatory to coupling up to a full trailer of steel for the return trip. Travelling in convoy with a colleague, Jed Lloyd, John was forced to stop because he felt unwell and by the time he arrived at the steel mills, he was parked behind Jed. Waiting to be off-loaded, the two of them sat in the cab of John's tractor (number 18), sheltering from the rain and chatting. "Are you alright, John?", asked Jed, "You're a bit pale".

Looking in the rear-view mirror John had to agree that he was a strange colour and Jed suggested that he saw the nurse. Pulling his truck out of the line, he drove over to the British Steel medical facility. The nurse was sufficiently alarmed by his condition to send him straight to Royal Gwent Hospital, leaving his truck outside the medical unit. By the early afternoon he was in intensive care and at 3.00pm that afternoon, John suffered a heart attack, from which he had to be revived. The heart attack had come on 18 February 1994 and John underwent a triple by-pass operation on 20 August 1995. Happily, he went on to make a full recovery, although it did put an end to his transport driving career.

His wife Mo suffered a similar attack in December 1995 but, sadly, she did not survive it.

After many happy years of marriage to Mo, and at the ripe old age of 64, John was not really seeking a new partner... but, he chanced to meet Sandra at Newport in July 1996 and they seemed to click. They married in July 1998 and Sandra has been a constant companion and a source of comfort and support for him since that time.

Even though he can no longer drive the heavy trucks that have been so much a part of his life, John maintains his interest in the family firm and in the heavy-haulage world. To this day, John retains the Wynns' company archive and is an enthusiastic custodian of the company's history. •

Scammell Highwayman draw-bar tractor coupled to a tanker trailer.

What is more interesting here than the Fordson tractor is the ex-WD 'Queen Mary' trailer to which it is coupled. Built by Taskers, these trailers were originally supplied to the RAF and were designed for moving aircraft fuselages.

Rare bonneted Guy Invincible tractor hauling a
Pettibone Super 70 log handler which is just a little too large for the trailer.

Guy Invincible 6x4 tractor, seen here coupled to a low-loader semi-trailer.

Another Guy Invincible, dating from 1960 and this time in rigid 8x4 configuration, carrying a large ship's propeller.

Carry that weight

Heavy haulage can easily be perceived as a romantic business, and one that is full of tales of 'derring-do'. But it is all too easy to be seduced by the charisma and romance of the tractor when the truth is that heavy haulage is as much about the trailer as it is the prime mover.

After all, the tractor simply provides sufficient grunt to actually move the load, whereas the trailer has to be capable of holding the load securely in place during the move, supporting the load's weight – a weight that's often very considerable – and providing the steersman with the facilities required to

The crew sit under the swan-neck of one of the Nicolas trailers, giving an excellent idea of scale.

Huge chemical vessel carried on a pair of Nicolas flat-topped seven-line bogies.

Nicolas seven-line bogie showing how the swan necks pivot on the bogie. The rear cab for the steersman can be seen on the left of the photograph.

help the tractor guide the load into position without incident.

In the early days of the business, a trailer was really nothing more than a platform on wheels. In the 1920s, for example, even the heaviest loads were carried on nothing more sophisticated than an extensible trailer running on a pair of solid-tyred axles, or a low-loader semi-trailer, again generally shod with solid tyres. As riveted construction gave way to welding, the carrying capacity of the trailers increased but the use of solid tyres was always a constraining factor and the heavy loading from the closely-spaced hard rubber wheels played havoc with road surfaces.

By the middle of World War 2 the girder trailer had made its first

When not in use, the connecting girders can be removed and the swan necks coupled together to ease the return journey.

appearance. Consisting essentially of a pair of separate bogies connected by a girder frame, this type of design was ideal for moving large transformers, up to 90 or 100 tons in weight. Loading and unloading were effected by using jacks to support the girders and, by carrying the transformer as low as possible in the girder frame, the stability of the outfit was improved because the centre of gravity was equally low. For other types of load of similar weight, the bogies could be used with swan-neck frames, an idea which been developed by 'HP' and which remains in common use today. Wynns' swan-neck trailers 300, 301, 302 and 303 were constructed using necks

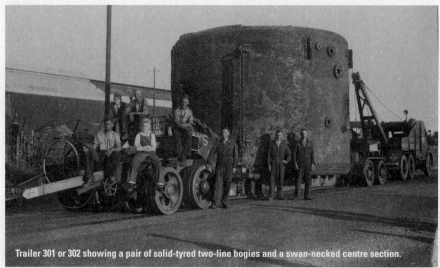

Trailer 301 or 302 showing a pair of solid-tyred two-line bogies and a swan-necked centre section.

A pair of Scammell Contractors, each hauling a single seven-line bogie unit together with the swan neck.

Trailer 261 was a simple drop-frame affair with solid tyres, typically used to carry railway locomotives or similar loads.

Sentinel steam lorry with a large enclosed semi-trailer.

and guides from Fairfields of Chepstow, whilst the bogies were built in Wynns' own workshops, at first using riveted construction for number 300, and then welded construction for the other three, all of them rated at 100 tons.

However, heavy haulage isn't just about supporting increasingly-large loads. It is equally important that the load can be manoeuvred on the road, both to clear immovable obstacles and to get the load itself into its final position. Separate rotating bogies had the advantage of allowing the use of a second, pusher, tractor to help steer the trailer in tight spots as well as assisting with moving the weight.

As the weights of loads continued to climb beyond 100 tons, the number of axles and wheels on the bogies was

Photographed in May 1950, this shows swan-neck trailer 300 after conversion to pneumatic tyres. The load weighs 81 tons.

A Crane-Fruehauf 300-ton trailer, consisting of a pair of six-line bogies and swan necks, undergoing trials before export to the Soviet Union.

similarly increased, but solid tyres continued to be the norm and continued to be a restricting factor. The problem was that pneumatic tyre technology had not advanced to the stage where pneumatic tyres were sufficiently reliable for heavy loads. Nevertheless, during World War 2, Wynns acquired at least one Cranes 40/50-ton 24-wheeled tank transporter trailer running on pneumatic tyres and this proved useful for a variety of loads and, despite the all-too common occurrence of punctures, it was probably this

trailer, with its three rows of pneumatic tyres, which showed that solid tyres probably had no future.

In 1948, the trailer manufacturers Cranes of Dereham started work on a heavy-capacity trailer which was designed from the outset to use a combination of large-section pneumatic tyres, together with an adaptation of the hydraulics systems used on aircraft landing gear to provide a form of suspension and steering, and an in-built jacking system. The pneumatic tyres greatly increased the ground contact area and reduced the possibility of damage to the road surface, whilst the

hydraulics could be used to maintain equal loading on each of the wheels. A new type of tyre was designed based on those used on earth-moving machines but rated for ten tons. With 16 of these 16.00-20 24-ply tyres Cranes engineers believed that a trailer would be capable of carrying 120 tons at speeds of up to 5mph.

A model was constructed and was displayed at the Commercial Motor Show in 1950 where it came to the attention of 'HP' Wynn... as well as Rex Faro, the latter from Wynns' great rivals, Pickfords. Back at Newport after his visit

WW2 ex-military 40-ton tank-transporter trailer doing what it was designed for; purchased at auction, these trailers formed a useful component of the mid-duty fleet. The tractor is also one of Wynns' ex-military Diamond Ts.

Trailer 444, consisting of a pair of three-line bogies on big Goodyear pneumatics and the swan necks, was eventually sold to Ulster Transport in Northern Ireland.

These days, transport companies who move outsized loads are allowed to provide their own escorts but back in Wynns' heyday the escorting was always done by police motorcyclists whose job it was to keep the public out of the way. The photograph shows trailer 444 before sale to Northern Ireland.

to the Show, 'HP' convinced his fellow directors that this was where the future lay and, stealing a march on the more bureaucratic Pickfords organisation, Wynns went ahead and ordered a 120-ton hydraulically-steered and suspended trailer from Cranes, based on the design of the model. The trailer, which had 16 wheels and was priced at £14,000 (more than £310,000 at 2010 values), was fitted with an auxiliary diesel engine to power the steering and suspension and to raise and lower the bogies, and had a steering position at the rear. The main frame girders were supported on swan necks bolted to the box-section bogie frames.

The trailer was delivered to Wynns in March 1951 and was used to remove the 105-ton North British Locomotive steam engine from the Festival of Britain site later that year. The trailer was given the fleet number 333 and should probably be considered to be the most significant piece of equipment acquired by the company up to that date. Despite the manufacturer's maximum rating of 120 tons, Wynns believed that the trailer was perfectly capable of operating at up to 150 tons and it was often used at this figure. In 1954 it was returned to Cranes for rebuilding and came back fitted with 40 wheels, arranged as two rows of eight and two rows of 12 wheels. In this form, renumbered as trailer 444 and rated for 200 tons, it was used to move a 120-ton stator from Stafford to Drakelow. The upgrading work had cost £12,000 which means that, in just three years, this trailer had cost the company £26,000 – which equates to more than £675,000 in today's money!

Despite its not inconsiderable price, trailer 333/444 more than earned its keep but technology moved on and, in

Trailer 302, riding on solid tyres, was used to bring the North British locomotive to the Festival of Britain. When the locomotive was removed from the site, it was carried on trailer 333, riding on pneumatic tyres.

Another view of trailer 444, loaded with an English Electric stator being moved from Stafford to Drakelow. Following a £12,000 rebuild at Cranes, who had originally rated the unit at 120 tons, the trailer was considered to be good for loads up to 200 tons.

1956, the bogies of 444 were sold to a company in Northern Ireland. The original frame of 333 had already been fitted with a pair of Cranes 16-wheel bogies (two rows of eight wheels) and had become trailer number 500.

In 1955, at a price of £18,000, Cranes supplied trailer number 555, a 24-wheeled hydraulic unit rated for 150 tons. This remained in use until the end of 1959 when it was sold to South America but, as the weight of loads continued inexorably upwards, 'HP' came up with the idea of adding additional castor wheels between the swan necks. This had ther advantage of adding nothing to the trailer length but allowed the load to be increased to 200 tons. Trailer 666 was thus equipped, whilst 777 was similar but lacked the castors. Later the frame of trailer 666 was fitted with a pair 16-wheel bogies to make trailer 456.

The company's allegiance to Cranes of Dereham ended in 1957 when trailer number 888 was purchased from the German company Scheuerle. Described

This huge steam drum for the CEGB's Littlebrook D Power Station is being carried on an assembled 10-line flat-top bogie and a seven-line unit.

Stanlow. At the time, these were the largest loads moved on British roads, but perhaps the most important trailer operated by Wynns was number 789, a six-line 48-wheel unit rated for 300 tons which was bought from Cranes in 1961. The bogies could be coupled together to form a flat-top unit or fitted with swan necks to make a bolster trailer and this unit was subsequently acquired by Abnormal Load Engineering (ALE). In 1966 this was followed by trailer 999, a Cranes-built unit rated for 300 tons and running on large wheels. Both 789 and 999 were converted to operate with the blower equipment developed by the CEGB to reduce the loading on bridges. The trailers were fitted with removable skirts and had ducts to a separate truck which was equipped with four huge eight-cylinder Rolls-Royce B81 petrol engines to generate lift. By March 1977, some 1,000 bridges had been safely crossed in this manner.

The development of today's sophisticated self-propelled modular transporters (SPMT's) came too late to play any part in the Wynns' story. But whilst these versatile units may have have transformed some of the aspects of the transportation of large and heavy cargoes, they owe their existence to much of the pioneering work done by, or under the direction of, 'HP' and his team at Newport.

rather disparagingly by Cranes' engineering staff, who had declined to quote for constructing the unit, as a 'roller skate', it used 16 small-diameter wheels to provide a minimum load height of just 36 inches and yet offered a capacity of 100 tons. Unable to design a trailer with more than 12 inches lift in the suspension, Cranes missed out

again in 1968/69 when the French company, Nicolas, produced a seven-line unit which managed 24 inches of lift. The seven-line bogies from this trailer, numbered 987, were used on the Stanlow refinery job where Wynns moved three enormous pressure vessels 17 miles from Cammell Laird at Birkenhead to the Shell refinery at

Today's modular trailer units enable the construction of a trailer to suit almost any size of load; the vessel is being carried on two bogies, one 10-line, the other seven-line, and is being supported on purpose-made load-bearing steel fabrications.

CRANE

L37   WYNNS

FDW
769E

Flashback...

Measuring 90 feet in length, and with a diameter of 17 feet, this chemical vessel was manufactured by John Thompson Horseley Bridge Limited and was on its way to Liverpool Docks for shipment to Canada. The method of supporting the vessel on a pair of bogies was chosen to reduce the overall height. The tractor is the 100-ton Scammell Contractor FDW 769E.

Made by
JOHN THOMPSON
HORSELEY BRIDGE LIMITED
Dudley

Concorde fuselage G-BOAA loaded on the *Terra Marique* passes the Houses of Parliament on its journey to the National Museum of Flight at East Fortune.

Water Wynns

The end of John Wynn's story is not quite the end of the Wynns' story. Although the company name had apparently disappeared back in 1983, there is a saying that 'what goes around, comes around'.

And so it would seem particularly apt that the name should have been revived for a heavy-haulage operation of a very different kind. But, to quote another well-worn phrase, 'that was then and this is now', and Robert Wynn & Sons which was the company that for so many years operated as Wynns Heavy Haulage, is now back in the hands of the Wynn family and being run by Peter Wynn, John's youngest son and the fifth generation of the Wynn family. But this is a completely different operation to the one that his Great Grandfather founded back in 1863.

Environmental concerns, growing traffic congestion and increasing red tape have all played their part in making

Concorde passing under Chiswick road bridge after being loaded at Isleworth.

The *Terra Marique* prepares to berth at Milford Haven during the dismantling and transport of equipment at the former Waterston refinery.

the life of the heavy-haulage contractor very difficult indeed. Sensing that the market was changing, and that the process of moving heavy and over-sized loads by road was simply going to become more and more difficult, Peter Wynn and his partners looked hard at the market and identified what has proved to be a profitable opportunity. The current Wynns' company does not own any heavy road tractors, preferring, instead, to work with haulage companies which have machines and equipment to suit whatever is the particular job in hand. This ensures that someone else jumps through those endless bureaucratic hoops.

These days, Robert Wynn & Sons' secret weapon is the *Terra Marique*, a towed sea-going barge that has been designed to handle abnormal indivisible loads.

This unique vessel allows both 'dry' and 'wet' loading. In the former case, the load can be brought onto the vessel via a dockside, riverbank or beach (as is the case when loading at Waterston) using specialised trailers that are simply rolled on and off the vessel across the huge loading ramp. For 'wet' loading, the load can be floated into the flooded cargo bay of the vessel on an inland barge. The *Terra Marique* is no toy... with a length of more than 250 feet, the 200-foot long hold can accept loads up to 1,350 tons, and sophisticated hydraulics allow the vessel to be bottomed, and for the deck to be raised and lowered, keeping it level with a dock or loading ramp regardless of the rise and fall of the

tide. And, although the vessel is primarily intended to be towed, a pair of Caterpillar 3508B 900bhp diesel engines, in conjunction with a hydrojet drive system, provide forward, lateral and reverse propulsion. The vessel is thus able to navigate inland waterways, such as the Manchester Ship Canal, under her own power.

The *Terra Marique* – the name is Latin for 'by land and sea' and is featured on the coat of arms of Wynns' historic home of Newport, South Wales – was officially named by Peter's daughter Daisy Wynn in the presence of David Jamison MP, the then Shipping Minister at the Palace of Westminster in April 2004.

View of the spacious loading area in the hold of the *Terra Marique*.

For her first cargo-carrying journey voyage, the *Terra Marique* carried the fuselage of British Airways' Concorde G-BOAA. World-wide specialist heavy-lift contractors Abnormal Load Engineering (ALE) delivered the fuselage on a 110-ton trailer by road from Heathrow to the Thames at Isleworth Quay where it was rolled onto the barge. The tail was removed to allow the fuselage to pass underneath overhead structures The first leg of the journey saw the *Terra Marique*, the largest vessel ever to navigate the Thames to Isleworth, pass under 25 bridges on its route through central London to Dartford, pausing briefly, for the benefit of the tens of thousands of well-wishers and the world's media, in front of the Palace of Westminster where the fuselage was raised on the vessel's hydraulic roadways. There followed a three-day voyage from Dartford up the east coast to British Energy's quay at Torness Power Station. Here, representatives of the National Museum of Scotland, British Energy, Wynns and ALE greeted her arrival. The fuselage continued by road to the National Museum of Flight at East Fortune.

If the load had been moved by road for the entire 400-mile journey, it would have had to be further dismantled, complicating the already lengthy process of reassembling the aircraft at the Museum.

Her second charter saw the *Terra Marique* become the largest vessel to navigate the River Trent up-stream of Gainsborough, when she transported a

Abnormal Load Engineering (ALE) used these self-propelled modular trailer units (SPMT) to shift parts of the Waterston refinery to the water's edge at Milford Haven. The operator walks alongside the trailer steering and levelling it via a hand-held console with a joystick control.

260-ton electricity transformer to the Cottam Power Station in Nottinghamshire. The vessel was awarded the prestigious Innovation award at the 2004 Seawork exhibition in recognition of both the concept and practical application of the design. Subsequent loads carried have included many huge transformers, electricity-generating equipment, two 500-ton 'toeheads' for offshore platforms, a Eurostar locomotive... and, of course, the pieces of Waterston oil refinery.

Perhaps the most fascinating project undertaken to date by the reincarnated Robert Wynn & Sons took place in South Wales, at the site of the former Waterston refinery... but first, a little history.

In the late 1950s, Esso constructed a large oil refinery at Herbrandston near to Milford Haven in Pembrokeshire. The refinery, which was the second such Esso plant to be constructed in Britain, opened in 1960, heralding the industrial and economic rebirth of the area. By 1974, Milford Haven had grown to become Britain's largest port in terms of ships, tonnage, and cargo, with four oil companies operating refinery plants in the area. One of these plants was located at Waterston, a mile or two inland behind the port, on the site of the ancestral home of Sir Isaac Newton. Originally constructed for Gulf Oil in the mid-1960s, it was latterly owned and operated by Petroplus, and then by Sem Logistics Tank Storage.

During the construction of the Waterston refinery, Wynns Heavy Haulage was commissioned to offload heavy plant and equipment from flat-top barges which berthed on a concrete

loading ramp constructed especially for this purpose at Milford Haven. John Wynn himself had been in charge of the project and, working in narrow windows of time dictated by the tides, a fleet of Diamond T and Pacific tractors hauled the heavy loads up from the water's edge, before continuing for a mile or two up the hill to the site where the refinery was being built. So it would seem particularly apt that the present incarnation of Robert Wynn & Sons should be involved in the removal of that very same plant and equipment 40 years later.

The Waterston refinery was closed in 1997 and for some years the plant lay abandoned. Planning consent was

ALE used massive Faun tractors to manoeuvre the load into the hold of the *Terra Marique*.

eventually granted to use part of the site for a natural gas terminal where the Malaysian company, Petronas, plans to ship liquefied natural gas (LNG) – gas cooled to liquid form to make it easier to transport – from all over the world. The old refinery was considered to be redundant and the obvious course of action would have been to demolish it and cut it up on site for scrap. However, in what many might consider an audacious move, the plant has actually been dismantled, rather than demolished, and has been sold to Pakistan where it will be re-erected and re-commissioned.

The refinery had been dismantled over a period of months, but it still consisted of a series of very large and heavy pieces that were not further divisible into smaller loads. All of the loads, the largest of which may well have been more than 300 tons in weight, had to be brought down the hill from the refinery site using either a towed trailer or a self-propelled trailer module, and loaded into the *Terra Marique*. The loaded vessel was towed around the coast to Pembroke Dock where the process was reversed, and the loads were left on the quayside to subsequently be reloaded into a heavy lift ship for onward transit to Pakistan. Although this may seem like a long-winded process, the alternative, which would have been to move the loads by road from Waterston to Pembroke, was out of the question. The distance between the two points is only around five miles but it involves crossing the Cleddau toll bridge on the A477 which carries a weight restriction, and any alternative routes would have hugely increased the distance travelled and would certainly have involved the removal of street furniture and the effective closure of already congested roads for considerable periods as the load was moved.

It was planned that four separate lifts would be required to move all of the refinery equipment, which probably totalled in excess of 1,200 tons. The work was contracted to the Stafford-based but international heavy-haulage company Abnormal Load Engineering (ALE), with Wynns acting as sub-contractors for the short sea journey to Pembroke. ALE owns some real heavyweight tractors, including the legendary Alvis-Unipower MH8875 that was originally built as a contender for the British Army tank-transporter contract in 2001. However, the towing duties on this project were handled by two types of tractor – most impressive of the pair was the 6x6 Faun Koloss, a Cummins-powered ballast-bodied heavy-duty prime mover, generally used in conjunction with an eight-axle flat-topped trailer. The other was a DAF 8x4 heavy tractor.

The real *pièce de résistance* of the operation was the use of ALE's self-propelled modular transporter (SPMT) units, which are able to move huge loads without requiring a tractor.

These four- and six-axle hydraulically-powered transporters are designed for moving large and heavy cargoes, and can be operated independently or assembled into any combination, in-line or abreast, to provide a support platform which matches the characteristics of the load

Cummins-powered Faun Koloss 6x6 tractor manoeuvring part of the oil refinery.

and the route. The unit can be hydraulically adjusted on the move to keep the load level and upright, and individual axles can be steered through a full 360° allowing the transporter to move forwards, sideways or diagonally as required. The hydraulic system required to perform these tricks is connected to a diesel-engined power pack that is carried on one of the modules, and the whole unit can be driven from a removable cab or by means of a remote-control unit, with the operator walking alongside or ahead of the unit.

In the same way that the advent of the steered-axle trailer revolutionised the movement of heavy haulage back in the late 1950s, these versatile modular

transporters have allowed the industry to take another quantum leap forward.

But, whilst the technology may have improved beyond measure since the days of the old Diamond Ts and Pacifics, the same degree of skill is required to inch these huge loads into position. One can't help but admire the men who make it all look so easy, handling loads which weigh hundreds of tons as though child's play.

With a history which can be traced back almost 150 years, it is no idle boast that Wynns remain 'pioneers in heavy haulage' and, as the company claimed all those years ago, 'whatever you have to move we will find a vehicle to move it'.   •

DAF 8x4 ballast-bodied tractor coupled to a pair of six-line flat-top bogies.

Epilogue: departed friends

The story of Wynns is as much a story of the men who made these incredible feats possible as it is the story of the machinery that was used.

During conversations with John Wynn over the months, many of his friends and colleagues at Wynns were mentioned and John was keen that we brought together the names of those he particularly remembers.

Owen George Wynn

One of the sons of Robert Wynn. Born 31 August 1894, died 25 September 1974. John's father – known as 'OG' – didn't really drive but his administrative role in the company was crucial.

Henry Percy Wynn

John's Uncle Percy, who was always known as 'HP', was one of ten offspring of the original Robert Wynn (1863-1923), son of the founder Thomas Wynn and Nora Small. Percy had been apprenticed to Fowlers and was a natural engineer, and a fantastic innovator – it was Percy who developed much of the specialised equipment which allowed the industry to grow. Percy was one of the five Wynn brothers who ran the company after his father died in 1923. For years, the young John Wynn was Percy's chauffeur, whilst Percy became John's mentor. Born 13 December 1902, died 7 May 1984.

'HP', 'GP' and Bobby Wynn

Robert Thomas Wynn

Named after his father, and for that reason always called 'RT' or 'Arty', Robert Thomas Wynn was born on 7 September 1892 and died on 5 October 1968.

Gordon Parkhouse Wynn

Born 13 May 1905, died 1 February 1978.

Ern Adams

A gang foreman at Newport, Ern was a generous, warm-hearted man, who would always help John out when it came to planning and estimating for contracts, never taking any of the credit and, often as not, allowing John to look like he knew more than he did.

Bill Hayward and Arthur Matthews

Bill Hayward

Arthur Matthews

Excellent drivers who taught John how to respect and control heavy machinery.

Oscar Thomas

Another member of the Newport heavy gang whom John admired.

Fred Manley

John worked with Fred, a foreman in the Newport yard, from the age of ten – "Forget your name is Wynn" Fred told him, and "listen and learn". It was Fred who suggested that the young John Wynn ask his father to pay him for his work in the yard – father was not amused!